ACTIVATING JOY

A 40 Day Journey to Rediscovering the
Meaning of Joy

JESSICA HURTADO

Copyright © 2020 Jessica Hurtado

All rights reserved. No part of this publication may be reproduced, distributed or transmitted in any form or by any means, including photocopying, recording, or other electronic or mechanical methods, without the prior written permission of the publisher, except in the case of brief quotations embodies in critical reviews and certain other non-commercial uses permitted by copyright law. For permission requests, write to the publisher, addressed "Attention: Permissions" at the website below.

Reflecting on The Word

www.reflectingontheword.com

Quantity sales. Special discounts are available on quantity purchases by corporations, associations, and others. For details, contact the website above.

Activating Joy / Hurtado – 1st ed.

ISBN 978-1-7357699-2-9

Library of Congress Control Number: 2020917817

Scripture quotations marked "BSB" are taken from The Holy Bible, Berean Study Bible, BSB. Copyright ©2016 by Bible Hub. Used by Permission. All Rights Reserved Worldwide.

Scripture quotations marked "ESV" are from the ESV Bible® (The Holy Bible, English Standard Version®), copyright © 2001 by Crossway Bibles, a publishing ministry of Good News Publishers. Used by permission. All rights reserved.

Scriptures taken from the Holy Bible, New International Version®, NIV®. Copyright © 1973, 1978, 1984, 2011 by

Biblica, Inc.™ Used by permission of Zondervan. All rights reserved worldwide.

Scriptures marked NKJV are taken from the NEW KING JAMES VERSION (NKJV): Scripture taken from the NEW KING JAMES VERSION®. Copyright© 1982 by Thomas Nelson, Inc. Used by permission. All rights reserved.

Scriptures marked NLT are taken from the HOLY BIBLE, NEW LIVING TRANSLATION (NLT): Scriptures taken from the HOLY BIBLE, NEW LIVING TRANSLATION, Copyright© 1996, 2004, 2007 by Tyndale House Foundation. Used by permission of Tyndale House Publishers, Inc., Carol Stream, Illinois 60188. All rights reserved. Used by permission.

Praise for Activating Joy

This devotional beautifully guides us on a path to seeking joy again. In these tough times, this devotional grounds us in God's truths while pointing us to the promise found only in Jesus. We are given practical ways to exercise and grow our faith, all the while finding joy in our everyday life. Jessica, thank you for sharing your insights with us. – Misty Valverde, Wife, Mommy, Blogger, Bible Study Lead

A must read for anyone struggling to find joy in the midst of their pain. It's beautifully written and gives practical, thought provoking activations at the end of each section. The questions helped the writings penetrate deeper into my heart as I had to sit and think of how the topic related to me specifically. We all, at some point, struggle with seasons of pain and I just love how this book helps to get focused back on what's important and examine the heart to regain true joy. I think it would be great as a group study as well. I was really blessed by it. – Joanne Renova, Recovery Ministry Leader, Bible Study Facilitator

Jessica's background in analytics definitely shows in this book. I think it will be a great resource, especially if you like to process your thoughts and learn by breaking down the read. I love the practical comparisons too. It makes it very relatable. – Denise Garcia, Marathoner, Bible Study Lead, Servant of the Lord

Joy is a choice! Jessica has done it again! If you are lacking in joy, get this book and invite joy into your life. Jessica takes us on a 40-day journey where all roads lead to joy! She shows how it affects us spiritually, physically, emotionally, and mentally. Her real-life examples, and even scientific validation, leave us with full confirmation that Jesus meant for our lives to be abundant with joy! She shows us how joy is a fruit of the Spirit, which is available to us all because of Christ's death, and His ascension to heaven, which gave entrance to the Holy Spirit to live in us and lead us. This book is another home run with plenty of inspiration and scriptural reinforcement regarding the power of joy. – Pastor Lystra A. Wilson, Inspirational Author, Editor, Speaker, Life Transformation Mentor, and Founder of Women Inspire Women, Inc.

Activating Joy is one of the first books to guide you through the practical methods of engaging more joy in your life. Each chapter has a theme verse that is carefully unwrapped in a way that pertains to everyday life. As you follow along the path you come to a section called Activation, which sets this book apart from others because it invites you to participate, now that is where the real adventure truly begins. As you activate these principles in your everyday life you will begin to cultivate an environment of joy. The more you participate the more the atmosphere around you will change. – Lawanda Martinez, Author, Speaker, Blogger and Board Member Life Builder Seminars for Woman

You are off to a great journey as you begin this 40-day journey and rediscover the meaning of joy. Jessica Hurtado invites us to walk daily with her as she shares revelation and insight into God's design for genuine joy.

This practical guide leads us to activate joy in truth. As we walk daily giving ourselves to Holy Spirit, He will continue to lead us into all truth.

Life has it's own rhythm that is some days more intense than others, yet God Himself is at the helm. We find in Activating

Joy a wonderful road map of discovery and wisdom in our journey to fullness of joy.

Psalms 100:1-5 (MSG) On your feet now—applaud GOD! Bring a gift of laughter, sing yourselves into his presence. Know this: GOD is God, and God, GOD. He made us; we didn't make him. We're his people, his well-tended sheep. Enter with the password: "Thank you!" Make yourselves at home, talking praise. Thank him. Worship him. For GOD is sheer beauty, all-generous in love, loyal always and ever.

You will have a time of wonder as He leads you along the path to discovering joy. Smile and laugh with Him as His love covers and keeps you in perfect peace.

Isaiah 26:3 You will keep him in perfect peace, whose mind is stayed on You, because he trusts in You. – Dr. Cathy Guerrero Founder, Life Builder Seminars

Contents

Introduction	11
Thirsty Souls	13
The Director	19
Instill in Us	23
Reverential Posture	29
Happy or Stress?	33
Heart Condition	37
Sorrow Gives Way to Joy	41
So Full	45
Do Not Waste the Trial	49
Heart and Mind	53
Declare then Establish	57
Seed Turned into Grain	61
Unwrapping A Gift	65
The "Why"	69
Fitly Spoken	73
Joy Through Hope	77
Joy in Purpose	81
My "Spotter"	85
Joy Through Faith	89
Comfort in the Promises	93
My Bag	97
Eternal Rewards	101
Alignment Births Desire	105
God of Hope	109
Heaven's Party	113

Freedom Brings Joy 117

Do Not Miss It 121

Enjoy Each Play 125

Happenings 129

Restoration Projects... 133

Love Them Anyway 137

Receive Your Inheritance 141

Bountiful... 145

It's a Strategy 149

Ah-Ha!... 153

Role Model 157

All Seasons Change 161

Flesh or Spirit 165

Mourning into Dancing 169

What Are You Ingesting? 173

Notes... 177

About the Author 179

Introduction

Activating Joy

A 40 Day Journey to Rediscovering the Meaning of Joy

As I endeavored to rediscover the meaning of joy, I learned that joy is not tied to conventional values often used to measure happiness. Joy is not tied to success and recognitions, family and relationships, how many date nights you have with your spouse, or how clean your home is (although these are nice to have). Instead, I found that joy is deeply rooted in our surrender to the Holy Spirit. It has always been tied to our ability to choose the Spirit over the flesh, our ability to discern which fruit we are operating from, and our alignment to the will of the Father.

If you have ever wondered why you physically feel the heaviness of your feelings, or wonder how your friends or family members are going through a trying season in their lives, yet seem content, then I want to invite you to journey alongside the Holy Spirit to rediscover the power of joy. As we journey through 40 days of joy, you will learn how joy has always been God's plan to bring balance to your life, not only in "good seasons", but in trying seasons too. Learn how joy directly influences unintended or secondary aspects of your life such as mental and physical health. You will discover new ways to rejoice while weeping at the same time, and how true joy is found in your alignment to God's will for your life.

As you allow the revelation of joy to enter your heart, you will learn to live in the strength it provides. You will realize it has never been tethered to what is happening in and around your life, but has always been connected to who Christ was, is and always will be. May you find yourself filled with an overflow of joy that spills over to all of those around you, and continuously walk in all of its fruit.

Now take out your pens, highlighters, markers, or whatever you use to take notes. I want to encourage you to circle, underline, and highlight whatever the Lord leads you to, as you endeavor to rediscover the power of joy. If there is a new revelation or a refreshing of something previously known, take note of it. Do not let the blessing escape you. My prayer for you is that through this book, your journey would be filled with God's love, His presence, His blessings, and His unending joy!

Thirsty Souls

"In that day you will say: " 'O Lord, I will praise You; though You were angry with me, your anger is turned away, and You comfort me. Behold, God is my salvation, I will trust and not be afraid; 'For Yah, the Lord, is my strength and song; He also has become my salvation.' Therefore, with joy you will draw water from the wells of salvation." Isaiah 12:1-3 NKJV

"'Therefore'" is an announcement that because of '*A*' you get '*B*'. It is a result of something that preceded it. Isaiah is praising God for being our strength and our salvation. Praising him for being one we can trust and not fear. He is the Lord who comforts us. As a result of these things (therefore), we can draw water from the well of salvation, with joy.

When we engage in something, we habitually do it with gladness or with distaste. We might not be aware we are doing it, but we are siding with one or the other. We are either happy to go to work, or less than happy going. We are either happy to make dinner or dreading the process. We tend to transfer our feelings onto what we are engaged in. Even while doing something sedentary, such as watching television, we can watch a show with excitement, or we can watch it with a sense of apathy, a sense of indifference. We are constantly engaged in something coupled with an emotion attached to it. We see this in our focus scripture.

Our focus scripture shows as we continuously draw water for our thirsty souls from the well that will never run dry, the well of salvation, we can do it with joy. Why? Because the judgment we deserved was turned away. When someone is good to you despite the penance you deserved, you become partial to them. You develop a fondness toward them. This is the joy that the Lord impregnates our hearts with when we are saved by His mercy and grace. Although we deserved less than salvation, He saved us anyway. Although we deserved punishment, He chose mercy. Those are worthy reasons to joyfully draw water from the well of salvation.

You may be thinking, "Ok, how do I actually draw water from the well of salvation?" It is quite simple, salvation through Christ Jesus. When we are saved, we receive the Holy Spirit. The Holy Spirit is the living water that flows from our hearts (John 7:38-39). As we continue to remain in him, the Holy Spirit will continuously quench every part of our thirsty souls. Let's not forget that joy is one fruit of the Spirit. When we receive the Holy Spirit, we also receive the gift of joy.

Where are you drawing your water from? How do you quench your thirsty soul? Is it through food? Alcohol? Drugs? Sex? Social media? Relationships? Today, you can come to the feet of Jesus and He will quench every area of your soul that continuously thirsts for more. His Word promises that those who drink the water He gives will never thirst again (John 4:14).

"Anyone who drinks this water [the things of the world] will soon be thirsty again. But those who drink the water I give [salvation] will never be thirsty again. It becomes a fresh bubbling spring within them, giving them eternal life." (John 4:13-14).

Recommended Reading: John 7:38-39

Prayer: Dear heavenly Father, thank you for being my source of life, my source of joy, and my source of refreshing every single day. I need you today and I know I will need you tomorrow to quench my soul from the thirst the world continuously creates. I praise you for showing me mercy when I deserved punishment. I praise you for your goodness toward me. I pray that as I thirst, I will never forget to run to the well that never runs dry. The only source that can truly satisfy my soul. In Jesus's name I pray. Amen!

> If you read this devotional and would like to receive the free gift of salvation, found through Christ, which will quench your thirsty soul, I encourage you to pray this prayer.

> Prayer of salvation:

> Dear heavenly Father, I come to you as the broken human being that I am. Forgive me of my sins. I am tired of running to the things of this world to satisfy my thirsty soul, only to find myself with an unquenchable thirst the world cannot seem to satisfy. Your Word says, "If you confess with your mouth that Jesus is Lord and believe in your heart that God raised him from the dead, you will be saved. For it is by believing in your heart that you are made right with God, and it is by confessing with your mouth that you are saved." (Rom. 10:9-10). I believe in my heart that Jesus died on the cross for me and was raised from the dead on the third day. I choose to lay down my way and the worlds way of doing things, and I choose you Lord. I choose you Jesus to be my counselor, my comforter, my protector, my friend, my guide, my wisdom. Save me from my life of sin. Save me from my life of brokenness and fill me with your love. In Jesus's name I pray. Amen!

Day 1 Activation

The world will continuously strive to create a thirst in us through different platforms, whether it's commercials we see on television, our feed on social media platforms, a bigger house, a slimmer waistline, a fancier car, a prestigious title, and so forth. However, all these things are fleeting and will wither and die along with the earth.

What areas of your life have you felt thirsty in that you have looked to things of this world to satisfy instead of the Lord? No condemnation here. We cannot heal what we cannot identify. List it here.

Now take your list of things to the Lord in prayer seeking His healing for these areas. How do you believe the Father wants to satisfy your thirst in these areas of your life? Describe.

Knowing His well never runs dry, how can you continuously draw water from the well of your salvation with joy? This will look different for all of us. (Hint: Think of how the Lord ministers to you.)

18

The Director

"The LORD directs the steps of the godly. He delights in every detail of their lives." Psalm 37:23 NLT

When someone is watching a new movie, they do not really know what comes next or how it is going to end, but the director of the movie knows every scene. They know how the movie will start, the climactic points throughout, and the ending well before the movie ever begins. Much like the director of a movie, the Lord knows what is coming next and directs the steps of the godly.

When we are aligned with the will of God for our lives, we are being driven by the desires He has instilled within our hearts. As we are driven by the desires birth by God's presence in our lives, every step taken is a step directed by the Lord. The Hebrew translation of godly means kind. To be kind is to be godly. Being kind does not have to be warranted, its inclusive of all, its showing those who do not deserve mercy from you, the mercy of God anyway. As our steps are directed by the Lord, He delights in every detail of our lives.

As a parent, I delight in the things of my children. When they take their first steps, I am delighted. When they speak their first words, I am delighted. When they do well in school, sports, or sharing, I am delighted. How much more does our heavenly Father delight in every detail of our lives? When we are aligned with him, every step we take is directed by him and the joy this must bring him can only be imagined.

The scripture says, *"He delights in every detail of our lives."* When we write the book, he delights. When we spread the good news, he delights. When we serve others, he delights. The Lord delights in you. He delights in your joy. He delights in your victories. Although we would want to think he only delights in all the "'highs'" of our lives, the scriptures states, he delights in *every* detail. "'*Every*'" means all things, both good and bad. Why? Because he already knows how the movie will end before it ever begins. He knows how to work all things out for our good. He knows the end from the beginning. He can take all the things the enemy meant to destroy us and use them as our footstool to take us to our next scene. He delights in every detail of our lives.

Is the Lord directing your steps? Are you showing others the kindness and mercy the Lord has been so gracious to freely give you? Align yourself with His will for your life and allow Him to direct your steps. Know that in every detail of your everyday, as he leads, the Lord delights in you.

"And we know that all things work together for good to those who love God, to those who are the called according to His purpose." (Rom. 8:28)

Recommended reading: Isaiah 46:10, Romans 8:28, Psalm 110:1

Prayer: Dear heavenly Father, the thought of you delighting in the details of my life is overwhelming. I pray Lord for complete surrender to your desires for my life. I submit my life and every step to your direction. Father, direct me. I surrender Lord. Amen!

Day 2 Activation

When the director of a movie says "action", the production of the movie begins and when he says "cut", the production is either paused or ended. Write down an "action" he is directing you to today. Remember progress is not made in leaps and bounds, it is made one step at a time.

Write down what God is directing you to "cut" from your life. Although we tend to associate "cutting" something from our lives as a loss but when directed by the Lord, it always produces blessings. What is He asking you to cut today? An addiction, certain language, a particular show, certain relationships? Press into him and allow him to gently direct your heart in this area.

How did taking "action" and being willing to "cut" bring you joy? If you are still waiting to receive this fruit, how do you believe it will manifest in your life through your obedience?

How do you think this has brought delight to the Father? Press in. What do you hear him saying? Do you see anything? Is it a song, a word, a picture? Take note of it here.

Instill in Us

"You haven't done this before. Ask, using my name, and you will receive, and you will have abundant joy."
John 16:24 NLT

Jesus is having a conversation with his disciples about his approaching departure from the earth. They have never asked the Father using His name because the Lamb has not yet been slain. The new covenant has not yet been established. The disciples are still perplexed about what Jesus is sharing. There is no revelation yet. The affirmation of the new covenant, that would allow us to go directly to the Father because of what Jesus did on the cross, has not yet come to pass.

In our focus scripture, Jesus was giving the disciples "insider" information. He was getting ready to tear the veil. We would now be able to bring our petitions directly to the Father, using the name of Jesus. Throughout scripture, Jesus is recognized as our intercessor along with the Holy Spirit (Rom. 8:34, 26). [Noteworthy, both were established post crucifixion and resurrection]. If Jesus, our intercessor, is telling us, *"Ask, using my name, and you will receive, and you will have abundant joy"*, then what are we supposed to be asking for that will give us abundant joy?

Psalm 37:4 tells us, *"Delight yourself in the LORD, and he will give you the desires of your heart"*. To delight, in Hebrew, means to bend toward or take pleasure in. If we are inclined toward and take pleasure in things of the Lord, He will give us the desires of our heart. So, does this mean God turns into a magic genie that gives me everything I want? Not quite.

This scripture, in the correct context, is telling us that as we bend toward the Father, He will give us (instill in us) the desires of our heart. Still confused? If we look at our focus scripture, we see that when we ask, we will receive (since we are asking according to His will for our lives – the desire He's birth in us), then we will have abundant joy. How? Our desires are now aligned with His desires for our lives.

As we seek the will of the Father for our lives, we begin to ask for those desires he's birth in our heart. If we are asking for the desires of our heart, that are now in line with His will for us, we will receive, and this will produce abundant joy. There is no greater joy than to fulfill ones calling and purpose while here on earth as set forth for us in heaven.

If you are walking around feeling unfulfilled and dissatisfied, can I challenge you to ask yourself, am I fulfilling my God-given purpose. Am I living out my calling for the Kingdom? If you have a void you cannot seem to satisfy, allow the Father to fill it. He will always give you more than you could ever hope for or imagine: *"abundant joy."*

Recommended Reading: John 16, Romans 8:26, Romans 8:34

Prayer: Dear heavenly Father, thank you for making a way for me. Thank you for giving me life-giving promises that birth new desires in my heart that align with your will for me. I choose to live out my purpose, my calling. May I continue to receive revelation of who you created me to be as I bend toward and delight myself in you. In Jesus's name. Amen!

Day 3 Activation

Common questions we all face as humanity are, "Why am I here? What is my purpose?" Let me assure you that you are here because you were created with a purpose. *"For we are God's handiwork, created in Christ Jesus to do good works, which God prepared in advance for us to do." (Eph. 2:10)*

There is no greater joy than to walk in our God-given purpose. As you spend time with the Father, begin to ask him to instill in you the desires of his heart for your life. What do they look like? Is he showing you a picture? Did you just remember a specific event? Is there something that stirs up your passion more than anything else? These are clues. What do some of these things look like? List them here.

Do the "clues" listed above look like what you would expect them to look like? Or, are they contrary to what you were expecting?

How does this grow you and/or take you out of your comfort zone?

What are some steps you can take toward beginning to live out your God-given purpose? Remember, progress is made one step at a time. List three steps you can take over the next week to begin to live out your God-given purpose.

Describe, in detail, the experience in discovering your God-given purpose. Have you encountered joy yet? Do not worry if you are thinking, "I'm nervous", "Excited", "Scared", and everything in between, joy will follow!

28

Reverential Posture

"Blessed is the man who is always reverent, but he who hardens his heart falls into trouble." Proverbs 28:14 BSB

In the Bible, reverent has two connotations, depending on the context of the scripture. One is to fear, the other is to honor, to be in obedience, to respect. Before we dive deeper into both interpretations, lets establish that this fear is not the type of fear the enemy brings. It is a healthy reverential fear of the Lord. Meaning, you want to live your life according to His will for you. You do not want to walk in disobedience to what he's called you to. Reverential fear - much like a child-parent relationship (He is our heavenly Father after all).

Blessed is defined as enjoying happiness or bliss; to be filled with happiness; blissful; joyful. Notice blessed is not defined by anything material, but by a state of being. I do not see a new car, a big house, or a large bank account balance defining joy. It is a state of being. How many rich and/or famous people do we hear have committed suicide? Absolutely tragic and a reminder that no amount of money or material things can bring the joy and happiness that can only be found in God.

Our focus scripture tells us, *"Blessed is the one who is always reverent."* How? Romans 8:28, *"And we know that for those who love God all things work together for good, for those who are called according to his purpose"* (ESV). The apostle Paul reminds us that we do not have to lose our state of contentment based on our circumstances (the size of our house, the size of our bank account, the type of car we drive, how we look, what type of job we have, etc.). Our happiness is found in the reverential posture we have toward the Father, knowing regardless of what our circumstances look like, He brings goodness out of all of it.

"But he who hardens his heart, falls into trouble." To harden means to make hard, set, toughen, desensitize, make less sympathetic toward. If we look at the story of the Exodus (the Israelites being brought out of enslavement in Egypt), we see the Lord brought plague after plague into the land of Egypt and all the while, Pharaoh's heart remained hard. Despite all he was witnessing, he remained hardened (set, desensitized, lacking sympathy) toward freeing the enslaved Israelites. Due to the Pharaoh's hardened heart, the angel of death swept through the land and all the first-born Egyptians (young and old) died that very night. *"But he who hardens his heart, falls into trouble."*

What are the lessons found in our focus scripture? If we posture ourselves in a respectful honoring manner, turned toward the will of the Father, we will find blissful joy and happiness knowing that He works all our circumstances out for our good. If we choose to harden our hearts toward the will of the Father, we can be sure that trouble will eventually follow.

Do you find yourself with a hardened heart toward a group of people, a neighbor, a circumstance, or even God himself? Turn to the Father, posture yourself with a reverential heart knowing that only He can bring you the blessings that you seek for your life. I want to encourage you today to position your heart in reverence to the Father. Allow the blessings He has for you to pour out into your life.

Recommended Reading: Exodus 5-11

Prayer: Dear heavenly Father, thank you for allowing me to stand in awe and wonder of who you are. I choose to receive all the blessings you have set out for me that fill me with abundant joy. I pray that you would soften my heart in any area that has been hardened. In Jesus's name. Amen!

Day 4 Activation

We have learned from our focus scripture and the lessons taught in the Exodus that a hardened heart opens the door to trouble. When we become calloused, we are indirectly allowing injustices around us to be carried out. Not doing something about a situation is the same as allowing it to happen.

As you spend time with the Father today, ask him to show you things that you have hardened your heart toward. What are some things you already know your heart has become calloused toward? What are new things you were unaware of that the Father is revealing to you today. God always reveals what he is ready to heal. List them here.

What is an action that you can take to counteract a calloused area in your life? This can look different for all of us. A simple phone call or a text message, or maybe it can start with the acknowledgment that something needs to be done. Remember, progress is made one step at a time. What can you do today to begin softening that area of your heart? Ask the Father and list it here.

How can you lean on the Father to walk you through this process? Rest in knowing he's longing to set your heart free from this. (Tips: prayer, worship, accountability partner, etc.)

Happy or Stress?

"A joyful heart is good medicine, but a crushed spirit dries up the bones." Proverbs 17:22 ESV

A quick science lesson about our bodies will help us better understand our focus scripture. All emotions are carried through our bodies via a tiny chemical messenger called a neurotransmitter. These messengers send signals to our neurons (our nerves) who receive what we are feeling. Every emotion we feel directly affects the brain. We have the frontal lobe (control panel) that monitors our emotional state and the thalamus (how our emotional state will be carried out). When we feel joy, our tiny chemical messengers' dopamine and serotonin (known as happy hormones) are released, and our brains receive the signal that goes directly into our nervous system (the body's electrical wiring).

Our focus scripture outlines joy as good medicine. How is it that joy is good medicine for us? When the neurotransmitters are releasing "happy" hormones (joy) our bodies are functioning without duress. Joy elevates our mood, releasing good endorphins, which lowers our heart rate and reduces stress. Lower stress levels lead to a boost in the immune system, which ultimately supports longevity. *"But a crushed spirit [the opposite] dries up the bones."*

What are some examples that could represent the opposite of joy? Stress, anxiety, depression, etc. Since our nervous system is responding to the transmitters being sent, whether good or bad, what happens when the signals are from a crushed spirit? The hormones released are adrenaline and cortisol (known as stress hormones). When stress hormones are released into our nervous system several negative factors are immediately present.

Blood pressure is elevated, which can lead to heart disease. Cortisol hormones block the processes of some of the body's functions, to include digestion, leading to several digestive diseases. Cortisol also turns off certain aspects of the immune system that fight infection, leaving the body vulnerable to virus and disease. Chronic pain, insomnia, and suicidal thoughts are also associated to anxiety and depression (triggers for our neurotransmitters to release more stress hormones)[9].

Although I am not a brain expert or an expert in all the intricate functions of the nervous system, I know that our state of emotion signals our bodies to react either positively or negatively (joy or a crushed spirit). What are you releasing into your body? Happy hormones or stress hormones? Bask in the joy of the Lord. Allow His medicine to continuously flow through your body that you may experience the rich and healthy life, He died for you to live.

"I came that they may have life and have it abundantly" (John 10:10b).

Prayer: Dear heavenly Father, your words are like medicine to my weary soul. I thank you Father for giving me all the answers on how I can live my best life. I choose the medicine of joy. In Jesus's name. Amen!

Day 5 Activation

Fun Fact: "Smiling can trick your brain by elevating your mood, lowering your heart rate, and reducing your stress. The smile doesn't have to be based on real emotion because faking it works as well."[4] – Diana Samuel, MD

I'm not suggesting we walk around in a fake sense of joy, God has given us the real thing, but if you find yourself stressed, simply smile and allow the Lord's intricate design of our bodies to do the rest.

Since smiling can trick our brain to release those happy hormones that do our body good, what is a memory that always causes you to smile. Recall it and write it down here.

What is something you can do for someone else that will put a smile on their face? No gesture is too small.

How did your effort to make someone smile bring both them and you joy? Describe.

How can you integrate making someone smile a part of your everyday living? Be creative. There are no wrong answers.

Heart Condition

"Rejoice with those who rejoice, weep with those who weep."
Romans 12:15 ESV

While joy is a state of contentment, rejoicing is a form of expressing that joy. In what ways do you express your joy? What causes you to celebrate? What brings you joy that must be expressed? What causes you to rejoice? This can look different for all of us. For me, it can be as simple as a pair of soft comfy pajama pants. They are judgment free; they never feel too tight and they wrap me in, what feels like, love every single time. I cannot help but rejoice every time I put a pair on. Your reason might not be as trivial as mine, but regardless of how significant or insignificant the reason is, the result is still the same – joy.

In our focus scripture, we are instructed to *rejoice with those who rejoice*. This really is not very challenging to do. Who does not love to celebrate with others, right? But what happens when celebrating with others is actually hard to do? What happens when you wanted the promotion they got? When your friend is now married, and you are still waiting on the Lord to send your Boaz? When they received the blessing you thought you deserved? You want to rejoice with them, but deep down inside you feel like you genuinely cannot. What gives?

In Jeremiah 17:9, we see outlined, *"The heart is deceitful above all things, and desperately sick; who can understand it?"* How did it get sick? Our heart is naturally bent toward the flesh because of the fall. It has been taught that material possessions, accomplishments, recognition, etc. are ways to be "happy". Many born-again believers have turned away from these notions; however, the heart is deceitful and thus needs to be guarded. This is because it determines the direction in which our lives will go in. It holds our attitudes, beliefs, aspirations, pursuits, etc. The healthy thing to do with a friend who is celebrating a blessing in their lives is to rejoice, as the scripture instructs. As we continuously guard our hearts, we will be able to genuinely rejoice with those who rejoice.

But what of the second portion of this scripture, *weep with those who weep?* The apostle Paul was not calling us to be sad when we see sad people around us, but rather to be filled with compassion to such an extent that we could join others in their pain. If we could partner with someone who has lost their child, is going through a divorce, failed a class, or has a prodigal child - we could bring them the love and comfort of Christ in the midst of their pain. We could, in a sense, weep with those who weep. When we carry the love of Christ in our hearts, we are moved in our hearts with the things that move him.

Is there someone you know who you can rejoice with? Is there someone you can journey alongside as they walk through a season of weeping in their lives? Reach out. No gesture is too small. We all need the love, comfort, and joy that can only be found in Christ.

"Rejoice in the Lord always: and again I say, Rejoice." (Phil. 4:4)

Prayer: Dear Heavenly Father, thank you Lord for reminding me this life is not meant to be done alone. I will rejoice with those who rejoice, and I will weep with those who weep. Strengthen me for both and strengthen me through both. In Jesus's name. Amen!

Day 6 Activation

As the scriptures show us, *the heart is deceitful and desperately sick.* Ask the Father to show you an area in your heart that has been operating under the guise of deception. Was the guise something you knew about or was it an unexpected revelation? Describe.

What can you do to keep this area of your heart healthy?

Reach out to someone you know is going through a season of rejoicing and someone going through a season of weeping. Describe how these actions have brought joy into your day and theirs.

Sorrow Gives Way to Joy

"So you have sorrow now, but I will see you again; then you will rejoice, and no one can rob you of that joy."
John 16:22 NLT

In this scripture, Jesus is speaking to his disciples about his impending departure. *"In a little while you won't see me anymore. But a little while after that, you will see me again" (John 16:16).* The disciples, not knowing what he meant, asked themselves what he could possibly be referring to. Jesus knew what they were thinking so he gave them the promise found in our focus scripture. *"So you have sorrow now, but I will see you again; then you will rejoice, and no one can rob you of that joy."*

"'So'", is a statement announcing a reason or a presumption that something must or has already taken place in order to bring forth what is to come. Since Jesus was going to be crucified; thus, leaving his disciples, they would feel sorrow. But notice the focus scripture says *"sorrow now"* indicating a specific space in time. *Now* is present, in the moment, not continuous. Then Jesus provides an interruption for the sorrow, *"but"*. The sorrow would lift from the disciples because the present (now) pain would be interrupted by his return (*"but I will see you again"*).

That interruption from sorrow is made available to us because of Jesus's resurrection from his death upon the cross. This resurrection makes a way for another promise given in our focus scripture, a celebration of joy. *"Then you will rejoice, and no one can rob you of that joy."*. Not only is Jesus giving us insight into the things to come (sorrow, hope, joy) but also an eternal gift that cannot be stolen. How is this possible?

If our joy is found in the resurrection of Jesus Christ, then how can this ever be taken away from us? It can't! It is a joy that cannot be stolen from us because Jesus's resurrection cannot be undone; therefore, our joy found in him cannot be taken away. Isn't that amazing! Yes, we will face sorrow in our lifetime, but there is always joy in the midst of our sorrow that can be found in Christ's return.

Is there something robbing you of your joy today? Are you in the midst of sorrow? Allow me to remind you that sorrow may be '*now*', but it is not everlasting. It will give way to the hope found in Christ, which yields joy in the midst of our pain. He is faithful! Trust him to give you joy that cannot be taken from you.

Recommended Reading: John 16

Prayer: Dear heavenly Father, I praise your holy and glorious name. Lord, thank you for making a way for me. You made a way for sorrow to give way to joy, a joy that cannot be taken from me. I love you Lord. In your precious name I pray. Amen!

Day 7 Activation

If our joy is found in the resurrection of Christ, it cannot be undone. As we hold on to this truth, we can quickly unveil the things we have allowed to rob us of our joy that were never meant to hold our joy.

What are some things, circumstances, or people you have allowed to hold your joy?

As you have identified either the things or people you have given authority over your joy, how can you purpose to keep these from stealing your joy another day?

We all go through seasons of sorrow, if you have not been touched by sorrow in your life, keep living, and unfortunately it will come. But be encouraged, Jesus reminds us that sorrow gives way to the joy found in him. What sorrow have you been holding on to that you need to give to Jesus? He wants to have an exchange with you: your sorrow for his joy. Make the exchange here through a written prayer.

So Full

"You make known to me the path of life; in your presence there is fullness of joy." Psalm 16:11a ESV

Our focus scripture states, *"you make known"*. To make something known announces that it is not yet revealed. It is not a knowledge that we already hold, but rather a knowledge that is discovered. The Lord reveals to each one of us the path of life, but how? There are references throughout scripture that outline the varying ways God does this.

"Trust in the LORD with all your heart and lean not on your own understanding. In all your ways acknowledge Him, and He shall direct your paths" (Prov.3:5-6). In this Proverb, we see that if we remove ourselves out of the equation (our logic, reasoning, circumstances, feelings, etc.) and trust and lean on the Lord, even when it does not make sense, even when it does not feel good, even when we do not see a way. *If* we trust in the Lord and acknowledge him in our decisions, He will direct our paths. The path of life is revealed to us as we lean on and trust in him.

When something is full, it means it cannot contain any more. There are no empty spaces left, it is complete. Our focus scripture tells us that in the presence of our Father, in the presence of the Lord there is fullness of joy, but how do we enter into his presence that we may experience a joy that is so full, we cannot possibly contain any more of it?

- *Let us come into his presence with thanksgiving; let us make a joyful noise to him with songs of praise!* (Psa. 95:2)
- *Come into his presence with singing!* (Psa. 100:2b)

These scriptures reveal, it is through thanksgiving and praise that you enter into the presence of God. It does not say it's through letting God know how bad your circumstances are. It does not say it's by begging him to bring you happiness. It does not say it's by letting him know you'll be happy when you are debt free or your kids straighten out, or your spouse changes. Quite simply, you enter into his presence through being thankful for all that he is, all that he's done, and all that he continues to do in and through you. Sing praises to the one and only God who is worthy of our praise. An attitude of gratitude expressed has the power to bring you before the King!

Have you ever noticed that it is when you are not complaining but rather carrying a posture of gratitude and thanksgiving that your spirit is elated? Many may not realize it, but that's biblical. This scripture shows us that in the presence of God there is joy, delight, and happiness in such abundance we cannot handle any more of it. His presence is manifested through our grateful countenance and praise.

Are you in low supply of joy today? Would you like to experience fullness of joy, not just today, but every day? Give God a shout of praise. Sing songs to him. Worship him. Acknowledge him in all your ways. Enter his presence with thanksgiving and receive the joy that can only be found before him.

Prayer: Dear heavenly Father, thank you that in your presence there is fullness of joy. As I walk according to your ways you reveal the path written out for me that leads to life. I embrace every single word you speak. Continue to direct my paths. I praise and worship you with a heart full of love and thanksgiving for all that you are in my life, all that you have done, and will continue to set before me. I praise your holy name. Amen!

Day 8 Activation

The scriptures reveal that fullness of joy is found in the presence of our King. They also reveal that we come into his presence when we are thankful and praise him. List some of the things you are thankful for.

Now that you have outlined all the things you are thankful for, shout praises unto him for all that he has done. Worship him. He is worthy!

Now ask him to *make known* to you the path that leads to life as you walk out each day. What are some things he has revealed to you? Write them down so you will not forget.

Do Not Waste the Trial

"Count it all joy, my brothers, when you meet trials of various kinds, for you know that the testing of your faith produces steadfastness." James 1:2-3 ESV

To count something means to acknowledge it. We give it validation by considering it relevant enough to be noted. In our focus scripture, James is asking us to count it all joy when we meet trials of various kinds. This is immediately counter intuitive. How could we possibly count it a joyous occasion when we are faced with varying trials? James gives us the answer within our focus scripture, *"the testing of your faith produces steadfastness."*

A trial can be defined as anything less than favorable that we can encounter throughout our lifetimes. Opposition, testing, hardships, difficulties, challenges; in a nutshell – trials are unexpected ordeals that are an imposition to our day-to-day living. How many of us encounter resistance and immediately begin to celebrate? I'd like to say I do, but I am guilty of being a frail human that absolutely needs the promptings of the Spirit to remind me to rejoice.

Although these may seem like impositions to our lives, we are to rejoice and here is why. They are a test of our faith; however, this test is not in vain. This trial/test produces steadfastness in us. To be steadfast means to be unwavering, resolute, truly committed. Trials of varying kinds come into our lives not to bring torment and pain, but to create in us an unwavering endurance that solidifies our faith with greater resolve.

Have you ever enrolled a fifteen-year old into a class full of five-year old's? No, and why is that? If they were kept in a place of familiar comfort, they would never have the opportunity to grow. This is a simple analogy, but quite literally, translates the scripture for us. The reason we do not live a "trial-free" existence is because our faith grows under the pressure of the trials of life. The olive does not produce oil until it is pressed, the grapes do not produce wine until they are crushed and the same is true for us. We will not know what we are capable of producing until we endure varying trials and grow in our faith through the pressing and crushing of life.

What is still dormant inside of you that will only be manifested through the pressing trials of this life? Are you an author that has not been pressed by life yet? Are you a motivational speaker that has not allowed the crushing to produce the gift within you? Are you a wife or husband after God's own heart that has not discovered your value yet? We are to rejoice during these pressing times knowing that God is working something in us through the hardships to birth something that would otherwise remain in seed form. Notice the scripture says *when* trials come not *if*; therefore, seize the opportunity for growth when it shows up and rejoice!

Prayer: Dear heavenly Father, thank you for concerning yourself with me and giving me opportunities to rejoice and grow. I pray that I would have the presence of mind to rejoice and allow the trial to do the work. I declare that every trial I encounter will never be a wasted opportunity but produce within me it's intended purpose. In Jesus's name. Amen!

Day 9 Activation

Recall a trial in your life that you now realize was not there to bring you pain or torment but to produce an unwavering commitment in what you hold to be true about the Word of God.

How did this trial turn the pressing of the olive into oil in your life?

Do you believe the oil would have flowed in your life if it was not for the trial you faced? Explain.

Who can you encourage with this truth today? Share your treasure and reach out to them.

Heart and Mind

"Anxiety in a man's heart weighs him down, but a good word makes him glad." Proverbs 12:25 ESV

Anxiety is a very popular word in our culture today, but what exactly is anxiety? The American Psychological Association (APA), defines anxiety as "an emotion characterized by feelings of tension, worried thoughts and physical changes like increase blood pressure"[10]. Webster's dictionary defines it as a, "nervous disorder characterized by a state of excessive uneasiness and apprehension, typically with compulsive behavior or panic attacks"[6]. Although these two definitions closely align with one another, note that APA includes a physical response (rise in blood pressure) beyond feelings of uneasiness. How is this relevant to our focus scripture? There is a heart and mind connection.

"Anxiety in a man's heart weighs him down." Individuals that suffer from anxiety disorders experience improper ups and downs that can cause high blood pressure, heartbeat irregularities, and even heart attacks. Has anything been weighing you down lately? Unease over your job, your next presentation at work, getting dinner on the table, raising your children, pouring into your marriage, or maybe your friendships? The many things life gives us an opportunity to worry about or feel apprehensive toward can be endless. However, our focus scripture also provides a balance to the heaviness that might weigh us down, a *good word*.

Medical professionals have taken to one of the most popular techniques used to treat anxiety, Cognitive Behavioral Therapy. This form of therapy helps the patient identify triggers that lead to negative thoughts, helps them to understand why they aren't rational, and counters them with positive ones[3]. If worry and unease are simply thoughts that can weigh a heart down (which, in a literal sense, can cause heart disease), a simple counter thought (a good thought or word) can bring gladness, joy, and delight. *"Finally, brothers, whatever is true, whatever is honorable, whatever is just, whatever is pure, whatever is lovely, whatever is commendable, if there is any excellence, if there is anything worthy of praise, think about these things"* (Phil. 4:8).

How exciting to see science catch up to the living Word of God! How much more should we be mindful of our own thoughts and ensure we are not only thinking positive thoughts but giving good words to those around us. Anxiety tends to be a silent battle so let us resolve to be kind to those around us not only in action, but also with our words. Words are powerful and we should speak life to those in and around our lives with every opportunity afforded to us.

"Death and life are in the power of the tongue" (Prov. 18:21a). Speak life!

Prayer: Dear heavenly Father, thank you for always giving us the cure to the things that ail us. I praise your Word, which is the best medicine I could hope for. I choose to speak life over myself and to those around me. I choose gladness over heaviness. Give me joy Lord. I choose joy! In Jesus's name. Amen!

Day 10 Activation

Since anxiety in a man's heart weighs him down, but a good word makes him glad, what are some promises found in the Word of God that shed light on anxious thoughts you may have. List those thoughts and then counter them with the truth of God's Word.

As you walk through your day, purpose to remember these promises. What are some ways you can remember these promises if anxiety tries to attack?

List a *good word* that aligns with each portion of Philippians 4:8 in your life.

Whatever is true – write something true

Whatever is honorable – write something honorable

Whatever is just – write something just

Whatever is pure – write something pure

Whatever is lovely – write something lovely

Whatever is commendable – write something commendable

If there is any excellence – write something of excellence

If there is anything worthy of praise – write something worthy of praise

"Think about these things" (Phil. 4:8). I urge you, in your life, think about these good things.

Declare then Establish

"Though the fig tree does not bud and there are no grapes on the vines, though the olive crop fails and the fields produce no food, though there are no sheep in the pen and no cattle in the stalls, yet I will rejoice in the Lord, I will be joyful in God my Savior." Habakkuk 3:17-18 NIV

The word "*though*" represents a resolute stance despite circumstances. The prophet Habakkuk is citing his resolute stance to rejoice in the Lord despite what his circumstances look like. *Though the fig tree does not bud and there are no grapes on the vine* – although I am not seeing any fruit spring forth in my life right now, still I will rejoice in the Lord. *Though the olive crop fails, and the fields produce no food* – although the provision I am expecting does not come through and the harvest is not bountiful, I will rejoice in the Lord. *Though there are no sheep in the pen and no cattle in the stalls* – although I do not yet see my business multiplying or creating provision, still I will rejoice in the Lord.

Our focus scripture is speaking on the lack of provision and the lack of bearing fruit. Though the business failed, though your child went astray, though your spouse walked out on you, though you were fired from your job, though the medical report wasn't good, YET I will *rejoice in the Lord*. How could we bear such unfavorable circumstances yet rejoice *in* the Lord?

To be *in* something indicates an inclusion. You are part of the Father, part of the Son, and part of the Holy Spirit. You are filled with joy when you are found *in* him. If you are found in him, you lack nothing.

Habakkuk goes on to make a declaration - *I will be joyful in God my savior*. When you make a declaration, you are announcing something that you are establishing. For instance, you might declare "I am starting dinner" before you establish it (actually start making dinner); or you might say, "I am going to the gym", before you actually establish it (head out to the gym). Establishing is in the doing, but it starts with a declaration.

What are you declaring today? Are you making life-giving declarations over your life and those around you, or are you declaring death and defeat? Despite the circumstance, despite the hardship, despite the lack – rejoice in the Lord! Where is your heart found today? Is it found in him or is it found in the circumstances that surround you? Purpose to seek him above all else! Receive the love, favor, and joy, he has set before you when you find yourself in him. Declare his promises over your life and the lives of those around you.

Recommended Reading: Proverbs 18:20-21

Prayer: Dear heavenly Father, I thank you for being my everything. Although the fig tree does not bud and there are no grapes on the vines, although the olive crop fails and the fields produce no food, I will choose to rejoice in you! In Jesus's name. Amen!

Day 11 Activation

We see in our focus scripture that Habakkuk made a conscious choice to rejoice in the Lord, despite circumstances. What are some circumstances you have faced that have given you pause when it comes to rejoicing?

What are some things you can do to remain joyful through trying circumstances? (Hint: See Day 10 activation for support.)

Since we know that declarations are followed by actions, what are you declaring over your life? Search the Word of God and list at least three life-giving declarations over your life you would like to see come to pass.

Seed Turned into Grain

"Those who sow in tears will reap with shouts of joy. He who goes out weeping, bearing a trail of seed, will surely return with shouts of joy, carrying sheaves of grain."
Psalm 126:5-6 BSB

Our focus scripture immediately sets a condition. If this, then that. If you sow, you will reap, but what does it mean to sow in tears and reap with joy? It actually sounds like a contradiction. The mysteries of God, many times, are contradictory to our natural mind. *If you lose your life, you will find it (Matt.10:39). Give and it shall be given to you (Luke 6:38). If you try to hang on to your life, you will lose it (Matt 16:25).* It all sounds like a puzzling contradiction. I believe that's why he also said, *Lean not on your own understanding* (Prov. 3:5). We are not meant to reason out God's Word with our finite minds, but he does want us to study and understand it so it will become revelation to us, enabling us to live it out in our own lives. So, what do we make of our focus scripture?

"He who goes out weeping, bearing a trail of seed." We have learned from scripture, that the Word of God is referred to as seed (Luke 8:11). If we bear a trail of seed as we go out weeping, according to His Word, we will reap a great harvest, which will, in turn, yield joy. Although it costs us something to sow the seed (plant the Word of God), the harvest it produces causes us to shout for joy. Many of us want to be victorious, but we ca not have a victory without a battle. We cannot have a testimony without the trial. Although we have wept through our trial, we have wept through our testing, we now shout for joy in our victory! We can now sow a trail of seed that could have only been

cultivated through our weeping. The seed that was birth in us, in the midst of our testing, found in the mercies of our great King, planted during our rescue can now be scattered to those who follow behind us. We go from *needing* rescue to *giving* rescue. What a harvest of joy!

It costs something to carry a mantle! It costs something to carry an anointing! It costs something to crucify the flesh, to die to self, daily! As we sow in tears – staying up late writing the book, doing the research for the sermon, missing the dinner with friends to put together the keynotes for our speaking engagement, surrendering the night at the movies to give to the church – it costs us something, as we sow the Word of God in our lives. But remember, "*[you] will surely return with shouts of joy, carrying sheaves of grain [your harvest].*"

When you testify about the goodness of God, when you scatter the seed that has been given, you are walking in your God-given purpose. There is no greater joy that can be found in all the earthly, fleeting treasures this world has to offer than to walk daily in your God-given purpose. Use all the trials you have conquered and testify of his goodness. Rejoice in sharing of his faithfulness. Sow the seed and reap the harvest.

*"Weeping may endure for a night, but joy cometh in the morning" (*Psalm 30:5).

Recommended Reading: Luke 8:4-15

Prayer: Dear heavenly Father, thank you for the battles that now cause me to shout with joy. I stand as a victorious warrior, resulting from each trying time. I love all of the seed you have placed in me. That seed can now be scattered in a trail for those who need to hear of your faithfulness, who need to hear of the victory that is surely to come, the testimony that will be birth. Thank you for your faithfulness Father. I love you and praise you. In Jesus's name. Amen!

Day 12 Activation

What is your testimony (your story of salvation; your story of breakthrough)? Write it down.

Scatter you seed. Share your testimony with someone you believe will be blessed by it, or someone the Lord leads you to share it with. Ask the Holy Spirit and you will get a sense of who he wants you to bless. Write their name(s) here.

Describe the joy that was found in the breakthrough, in the victory. If you are still in the midst of the battle, rejoice in knowing that although you sow with tears, you will reap with shouts of joy. What does this look like for you?

Unwrapping A Gift

"Your promises are the source of my bubbling joy; the revelation of your word thrills me like one who has discovered hidden treasure." Psalm 119:162 TPT

Have you ever experienced "bubbling joy"? If you have not, you will know it when it shows up. It's an excited child on Christmas day, discovering that Santa visited their home while they slept – bubbling joy. It is holding your child in your arms for the first time – bubbling joy. It is witnessing your child take their first steps – bubbling joy. Watching your child graduate – bubbling joy. Your wedding day – bubbling joy. The salvation of your loved ones – bubbling joy. Although these all seem to be life milestones, bubbling joy can also be found in the everyday living too. The first sip of coffee you have every morning – bubbling joy. Watching a beautiful sunset after a fulfilling day – bubbling joy. The perfect conversation with your best friend – bubbling joy. The innocent laughter of children – bubbling joy. So, how is joy any different from bubbling joy?

Joy is a state of contentment and delight, while bubbling joy has the added benefit of increasing to such an intense and immense caliber that you cannot keep it from "bubbling over" – like a boiling pot of water that overflows. It has nowhere to go but out. You feel joy at such an intense level that you simply cannot hide it, even if you tried, but why would you?

In our focus scripture, David's source of bubbling joy are God's promises. He goes on further to state, the revelation of God's promises thrills him. To reveal something means it unfolds before you. It is like a Christmas present, it is already there (under the Christmas tree or in your stocking), but its contents have not yet been revealed to you, until the appointed time (Christmas day). The same is true with the Bible. Its content (scripture) sits before us, but the revelation is for an appointed time. God's Word has the power to bring bubbling joy as it is revealed to us. It is like the thrill of unwrapping a present – hidden treasure in plain sight.

"It is the glory of God to conceal things, but the glory of kings is to search things out." (Prov. 25:2)

Prayer: Dear heavenly Father, thank you for the bubbling joy you bring into my life every day. Thank you for all the moments you have given me in my lifetime that have been filled with bubbling joy. I am so glad to know your Word is my daily source of bubbling joy. Continue to reveal to me your promises that I may be filled with the thrills that can only be found in you. In Jesus's name. Amen!

Day 13 Activation

What causes you to experience bubbling joy?

How can you bless someone today by stirring up bubbling joy in them? (Knowing their love language could be helpful, but not necessary.)

What can you gain from learning what brings you into a state of contentment regardless of circumstances?

What is a *"revealing"* you have been believing for from the Father? This can be anything you have been expectantly awaiting a response for. Remember you have not because you ask not. Ask now.

The "Why"

"I will greatly rejoice in the LORD, my soul shall be joyful in my God; for he hath clothed me with the garments of salvation, he hath covered me with the robe of righteousness." Isaiah 61:10a. KJV

Have you ever decided to do something and were determined about it, but when it was time to follow through it was harder than you had anticipated? Sunday night, you were determined to go to the gym on Monday, but Monday came around and the blankets were just too cozy to give up. You were determined to start your diet after the holidays, but the holidays came and went, and your eating habits did not change. Perhaps you were determined to take your family out over the weekend, but the couch was calling your name all weekend long. You want to start going to church, but you really do not feel like it on Sunday mornings. I am sure we have all encountered a time or two in our lives when we were determined to do something, but the follow-through was a lot more challenging than we had hoped. How can you get over this slump when you find yourself in it from time to time? Choose to remember your reason – the why.

The prophet Isaiah was making a declaration about something he had determined to do: *"I will...", "my soul shall...".* These are statements of a determined mind that has chosen to do something. But the prophet Isaiah follows those set decisions with the reasons why he was determined to rejoice and be joyful. He reflected on the things the Lord had done for him that caused him to rejoice and feel joyful in the first place. The Lord had clothed him with salvation and covered him with righteousness (right standing with God). The Lord was his superhero.

When we set out to do something but allow our feelings to dictate our outcome, we may never see our dreams and goals come to pass. You want to go to the gym because you want to be healthy and gain more energy – the why. You want to start your diet, not because you are obsessed with your weight, but because you want to live a healthier lifestyle – the why. You want to take your family out on the weekend, not because you are bored, but because you want to create priceless memories with each of them before these moments pass you by – the why. Your church attendance is not to appease what others might think of you, but rather to gather with other likeminded believers, to worship God and continue to grow in pursuit of him. You are more likely to follow through with your set declarations if you refocus your attention on the reasons *why* you endeavored to pursue those things to begin with.

I will greatly rejoice in my Lord because I know the pit he brought me out of (fill in your reason here). My soul shall be joyful in my God because he has loved me unconditionally through it all (fill in your reason here). Determine to remember why you rejoice and then remain joyful in him. If you do, when he calls you to your next assignment, you will not hesitate to pursue it will all diligence.

"Whatever your hand finds to do, do it with your might." (Eccl. 9:10)

Prayer: Dear heavenly Father, I will rejoice in your name. Thank you for giving me salvation and righteousness; two things I could never have gained on my own. I praise you and live in remembrance of all that you have done for me. I joyfully lift up your precious name. Amen!

Day 14 Activation

Recall a time in your life when you set a goal for yourself to achieve. Did you successfully attain it? Were you ever tempted to quit? What kept you going?

What is a declaration you have spoken over your life that you want to pursue? If you've never made one before, do so here.

As you set out to pursue your declaration, hold on to your "why". This will serve as a reminder, through all the obstacles that might present themselves, as you strive toward your goal, why you set out to achieve them. List your *why* here.

Fitly Spoken

"Everyone enjoys a fitting reply; it is wonderful to say the right thing at the right time!" Proverbs 15:23 NLT

Our focus scripture highlights how everyone enjoys a fitting reply, but what exactly is a fitting reply? Does that mean it is honest and straightforward? Not exactly. So how is it that an honest, straightforward and right answer is not necessarily a fitting response? All of these seem to be proper, but in the context of this scripture, a "fitting" response more closely aligns with the words appropriate or suitable.

How many of us have heard of a filter? I am sure most of us have. It is meant to remove impurities and to keep things out that could contaminate the things you are trying to keep or make pure. Although typically associated with water, it can also be used in the context of someone's speech. Children are a great example of having no filter. They have not usually developed the frame of mind yet to clean up their responses, in order to appease those around them or to sound polite. They are extremely transparent and give honest opinions when expressing themselves. If children lack a filter, it seems acceptable within society, cute even, but lacking a filter as an adult – not so cute.

Have you ever had or currently have a friend who does not have a filter when they speak? We all know of at least one person who lacks a filter when interacting with others. Does it ever feel awkward or even embarrassing to you when they give a response that is completely unfiltered? Why is that? The answer is in our focus scripture! Because *everyone enjoys a fitting reply; it is wonderful to say the right thing at the right time.* The New King James Version says it this way, *"A man has joy by the answer of his mouth, and a word spoken in due season, how good it is!"*

Everyone wants to say the right thing at the right time because it brings joy to them and those around them. We feel this sense of happiness and delight, knowing we brought that same feeling to those receiving our words. Are you stirring up feelings of awkwardness and discomfort when you speak or are you stirring up joy and delight? I challenge you to be intentional with the words you speak. Allow the Holy Spirit to be your filter. He will ensure all impurities are removed before you give your response. He will guide you to speak the right thing at the right time every time.

"A word fitly spoken is like apples of gold in settings of silver." (Prov. 25:11)

Prayer: Dear heavenly Father, thank you for the wisdom you knew I would need in my life before I ever knew I would need it. Thank you for giving me a word to speak in due season. I pray the Holy Spirit would continue to filter every word I speak and that I would be a constant source of fitting responses to those around me. In Jesus's name. Amen!

Day 15 Activation

We see that a word fitly spoken has the power to shift the atmosphere. Not just ours but those around us as well. *<u>Everyone</u> enjoys a fitting reply.* How can you intentionally shift your atmosphere today with the words you speak?

The second portion of our scripture reminds us, *"it is wonderful to say the right thing at the right time"*. How can this statement be applied with more intentionality throughout your day?

How can the Word of God help you make this a habitual way of living? Keep in mind, it takes approximately two months to form a new habit. So, do not expect things to shift overnight, but remember progress is made one step at a time.

Joy Through Hope

"Rejoice in hope, be patient in tribulation, be constant in prayer". Romans 12:12 ESV

The prefix "Re-" is defined as returning to a previous condition, a restoration. Joy is a state of being content, having delight. Our focus scripture indicates that we should *rejoice in hope*. If joy means to be content and re- means to return, then rejoice is telling us to return, be restored, in our contentment through hope. What happens when what we are hoping for has not yet come to pass? The remainder of our focus scripture give us the answer.

"Be patient... pray." We are called to be patient in all circumstances (both favorable and unfavorable). This statement does not say *'if'* we face tribulation but rather it assumes we *will* encounter it. We are to be patient when we are feeling under pressure, when we are unsure, when we cannot seem to see a way, when we have to trust God will work it out. When trials and pain enter our lives, we are to remain patient, and not lose our joy (which is kept through our hope). Lastly, pray.

To be constant in prayer means you are unending in your conversation with God. It is a continuous, relational communication. The trial might not be pleasant, and the circumstance may attempt to steal your joy, but if the antidote is to be unrelenting in conversation with the Father (prayer) while rejoicing in hope, the trial then becomes less magnified in your life.

Do you need to get your hope back? Do you need to rejoice (be restored to joy)? Be patient. Be constant in prayer.

Trust. Keep hoping for the cherished things God has placed in your heart. Everything in Christ is "Yes" and "Amen".

"For in this hope we were saved. But hope that is seen is no hope at all. Who hopes for what they already have?" (Rom. 8:24)

Recommended Reading: 2 Corinthians 1:20

Prayer: Dear heavenly Father, thank you for reminding me to return to joy through hope. To be restored to the confident expectations of the desires you have placed in my heart. I decree a double portion of patience and a supernatural thirst to seek you in prayer. In Jesus's name. Amen!

Day 16 Activation

Our heart longs for the things we desire, but as time passes and the fulfillment of these things seem delayed, according to our expectations, our hearts can grow weary. I want to encourage you to get your joy back by returning to hope.

In what areas of your life do you feel you have lost sight of hope?

What steps can you take today that will give your heart a refreshing of hope for the things you long for?

What does scripture say about the things we hope for that we have not yet received? (Hint: Romans 8:24) List as many as you choose.

How does a refreshing of hope stir up your joy?

Joy in Purpose

"If one member suffers, all suffer together; if one member is honored, all rejoice together." 1 Corinthians 12:26 ESV

The apostle Paul is teaching that as members of the body of Christ, we are all one body. We are to function and move as one in the Spirit just as the physical body does. No member or part of the body is more important than the other they simply each have their own unique intended function. He goes on to explain how the foot does not feel like they are not part of the body because they are not hands. Or how the ear does not feel like it is not part of the body because it is not an eye. They are both equally a part of the body. Each part is meant to function in its own capacity. This is true for believers as well. They are meant to function within their respective roles within the body of Christ.

Our focus scripture explains that if one member suffers, we all suffer. Have you ever noticed that if you get a headache your whole body suffers? It is not that your hands and feet hurt, or your eyes and ears hurt, but because your head is a part of the body, your body suffers as a whole. The same is true with the body of Christ. If a part of the body is not functioning as intended, the whole body of Christ suffers. If you had the feet trying to do what the hands do, the body would become inefficient. If you had the eyes trying to hear and the ears trying to see, you would not be able to see or hear.

If one member is honored, all rejoice together. We are not called to be envious of what others have or in what capacity they are functioning in. We are called to rejoice together when one member is honored. We are called to celebrate the mountain tops with them. No one member serves in a role more important than the other. Some roles may have more visibility than others, yet both are equally as important to the overall functionality of the church. Just like you cannot see the heart outside of the body, as its internal role is not on display, yet it is critical to the body's well-being and functionality. The same is true with the body of Christ. Even if you are not the one on the platform, even if you do not have a microphone in your hand, your part is still vital to the well-being of the entire body.

So, what does any of this have to do with joy? We find true joy and contentment when we learn to embrace the place where God has called us to serve. We are filled with joy and contentment when we realize which body part we are meant to function as. Some of us are called to be the hands and feet, while others are called to be the eyes, ears, and mouth. We are all uniquely different and all intricately intertwined to the overall function as the body of Christ.

"All of you together are Christ's body, and each of you is part of it." (1 Cor. 12:27)

Recommended Reading: 1 Corinthians 12:12-27

Prayer: Dear heavenly Father, I thank you for making me uniquely to function in the areas you have gifted me in. Keep strife and dissention far from me. Allow me to overflow with joy as I move in my intended function alongside others. I praise you Father. In Jesus's name. Amen!

Day 17 Activation

As you reflect upon these truths found in the Word of God, what part of the body of Christ do you feel you have been called to function in? Are you compelled to open your doors to others and extend hospitality? Are you driven to pray and intercede for the church and others? Do you have a gift of singing? We have all been gifted in an area. What body part do you identify with and why?

As you are discovering or reaffirming your function within the body of Christ, how can you serve those around you in your area of gifting?

You have identified the areas in which you can serve, if you are not serving already, I want to challenge you to take the next step. Get connected with a good, bible-based church and seek ways to serve. It might be a bit unnerving at first, but you will not regret it. List the steps you will take today to reach out and serve.

How did engaging in one or more of these steps today feel? Exciting, scary, joyous?

My "Spotter"

"What joy for those whose strength comes from the Lord, who have set their minds on a pilgrimage to Jerusalem."
Psalm 84:5 NLT

Have you ever gone to the gym to lift and needed a "spotter"? For those of you thinking, *"the only things I lift are donuts, and what is a spotter"*, I got you covered. A spotter is, essentially, a helper, only used as needed, when lifting/pushing heavy weight. You lift your weight and they "spot" you as you lift the weight to ensure the weight does not overpower (crush) you as the weight gets heavier. They typically stand in a vicinity far enough to allow you to successfully execute your motion, but close enough to step in if you need assistance. Although, typically, you may not be able to lift or push a certain amount of weight, with the assistance of a spotter, you can. This is what our life looks like when our strength comes from the Lord.

You may not be qualified to write the book (lift the weight), but with the Lord as your "spotter", you can. You may not be qualified to hold the microphone and stand on the platform (lift the weight), but with the Lord as your "spotter", you can. You weren't supposed to get out of the projects, you weren't supposed to buy your own home, you weren't supposed to live debt-free, but with the Lord as your "spotter", you are out of the projects, own your own home, and are living debt-free. When you allow the Lord to become your spotter, when the Lord is helping you lift the weight that is too heavy for you to bear on your own, when you have allowed him to support the weight, ensuring it does not crush you, that is when he has officially become the source of your strength. Although he never leaves us, he is far enough to allow us to *choose* to lift the weight (write the book, preach the sermon, live debt-free, etc.), but close enough to ensure the weight does not crush us. He is the source of our strength.

According to our focus scripture, if the Lord is the source of our strength (our "spotter"), it creates joy. But this joy is coupled with a mind that is set on a pilgrimage toward Jerusalem. So, what does that mean? One translation of Jerusalem is the city of peace. It is a spiritual journey toward peace, a journey toward God. I want to encourage you today to journey toward God, journey toward peace and encounter the joy that is found in the strength of the Lord along the way.

"O Lord of Heaven's Armies, what joy for those who trust in you." (Psa. 84:12)

Prayer: Dear heavenly Father, thank you for loving me with such depth that you will not allow anything to crush me. Thank you for being my source of strength. Thank you for creating joy in me as I continually journey toward you. I praise you. In Jesus's name. Amen!

Day 18 Activation

Like everything in your life, you have a choice to "lift" the assignments the Lord has given to you. When you feel you do not have what it takes, when you feel unqualified for what he is calling you to, remember, you are operating out of the Lord's strength and not your own.

What are some things in your life that you now realize were possible, not by your own might and power, but by the supernatural strength found through the Lord?

What assignments is he calling you to that you feel are "too heavy" to lift?

How will the assignments listed above become possible when you begin to lean on the strength of the Lord and not solely your own?

The focus scripture reminds us that as we journey toward peace, we will encounter joy. How do you see yourself encountering joy as you journey toward your assignment with the peace that God is your "spotter"?

Joy Through Faith

"Though you have not seen him, you love him; and even though you do not see him now, you believe in him and are filled with an inexpressible and glorious joy..."
1 Peter 1:8 NIV

The word "*though*" represents a stance despite circumstances. Peter is outlining for us that we are clearly not moved by sight (our circumstance), but by faith. Even though we do not or have not physically seen Jesus, we love him, we believe in him, and because of our faith and love toward him, we have an illogical joy that is a direct result of our faith.

There are many things that cannot be seen, yet we believe in their existence. Have you ever physically seen one hundred million dollars in person? Maybe not, yet its existence is still real. Have you ever physically seen air? No, yet its existence does not change. Why? Although you cannot physically see these things, the effects they have on your daily living are very real. Millions of dollars are interchanged in the business world every day for us to have and enjoy the commodities that are accessible in our lives (food, water, electricity, gasoline, shelter, transportation, etc.). The millions of dollars exchanged may not be physically seen by us, but the interchange is taking place just the same. The air cannot be seen, but its effects can be felt. You can see the wind blowing the leaves on trees, you can feel the wind touching your skin or moving your hair, yet you cannot see it. This is the case with the trinity (Father, Son, and Holy Spirit).

You may not have ever seen the Father, the Son or the Holy Spirit, but you feel their presence, you experience their promptings. You witness their favor and grace over your life.

Although they might not physically be seen, their effects can be seen and felt in our lives and the lives of those around us.

In our focus scripture, Peter is talking about the inexplicable joy that cannot be reasoned through our logic but can be felt because of our faith in Jesus. The inexplicable joy found in believers cannot be physically seen (as in you cannot go to the store and buy a jar of joy), but the effects can be seen and felt by us and those around us.

Do you have joy inexplicable? Do others see the affects the love of Jesus has on your life? Does your faith cause others to experience things that cannot be physically seen or logically explained but can be felt? I want to encourage you today to be the radiant joy that is desperately needed in our world today. Find yourself in trust unshakable bound by the joy produced through your faith in Christ Jesus.

Then Jesus told him, "You believe because you have seen me. Blessed are those who believe without seeing me." (John 20:29)

Prayer: Dear heavenly Father, thank you for giving me access to inexplicable joy that can be found through my belief in you. Although I may not always see you, I can always feel your presence in my life. I can always feel your love, favor, and your gentle correction in my life. I praise your Holy name. Amen!

Day 19 Activation

Recall a time in your life when you experienced the presence of God. Perhaps at the time you did not recognize it as such, but as you reflect on that moment now, describe your experience and how you know it was the beloved presence of God.

How did this moment make you realize that, although you cannot see him, you can feel and see God's effects in your life?

How has that encounter changed your life or the way you view the world around you?

Comfort in the Promises

"In the multitude of my thoughts within me thy comforts delight my soul." Psalm 94:19 NKJV

Have you ever heard the expression "the mind is the battlefield"? This expression implies that our minds have the ability to enable a battle within us. Since our minds have the ability to enable a battle, shouldn't they also have the ability to disable one? Our focus scripture gives a glimpse of what this can look like. Notice the scripture says, "*my* thoughts". "'*My*'" implies a form of ownership. We have tens of thousands of thoughts a day, but we do not have to take ownership of them all.

Let's break our focus scripture down. A multitude indicates a crowd or a large host; therefore, a multitude of thoughts basically means there are a lot of them. You have to pay the bills, get the kids to school, figure out what's for dinner, finish the project, remember if you put the clothes in the dryer before you headed out, wonder why they have not returned your text, check how many people liked your post, and so on. Thoughts are a part of everyday living; however, these thoughts are not meant to burden or overwhelm us (enable a battle). We can make a decision to think certain things on purpose.

The focus scripture further outlines that, of the many thoughts within us, the thoughts turned toward the Lord bring joy to our souls. So, how do we keep this *multitude* of thoughts in our minds from overwhelming us and instead turn them toward the Lord? "*Thy comforts*" ...

The Lord's comfort has the power to bring delight to our soul. What are some things that come to mind when you think of comfort? Maybe a warm blanket, a nice cup of coffee, chocolate, a slice of pie or cake, a hug, a song, a scripture, a word in season, or hearing, "It's going to be ok." Comfort looks different for all of us. We serve a God who uniquely custom makes the comfort we each need which creates delight within us.

Our soul, which includes our mind; thus, our thoughts, is enveloped in joy as the comfort of the Lord quiets our very busy minds. The *multitude* attacking our minds can be overpowered by entering the delight found in the Lord when we take refuge and comfort in him. I encourage you to take inventory of your thoughts today. What kind of thoughts are you taking ownership of? When the battle of the mind ensues seek the refuge that the Lord's comfort brings – comfort found in his promises. As our thoughts are turned toward him, he brings us comfort and delight.

"You keep him in perfect peace whose mind is stayed on you, because he trusts in you." (Isaiah 26:3)

Prayer: Dear heavenly Father, thank you for the many delights you bring to my soul. The comforts that can only be found in your arms. I cannot help but be met with joy. Keep my mind stayed on you that I may dwell within the covering of your peace. In Jesus's name I pray. Amen!

Day 20 Activation

There are so many fun facts about the mind/brain. Did you know that reading out loud actually promotes brain development, or that yawning helps cool down your brain? It's true, sleep deprivation raises the brains temperature so go ahead and yawn when you are tired, it cools off your brain[1].

The mind naturally wanders when the brain is at rest, so it is important to be aware of our own thoughts and keep them aligned with the Word of God. In what areas of your life have you allowed your mind to wander?

How has your wandering mind affected your life? (Ex.: anxiety, worry, hurt, strained relationships, etc.)

Since a wandering mind is a natural inclination of our bodies, how can you keep yourself accountable regarding your thoughts throughout each day? Hint: Reference Isaiah 26:3 and Philippians 4:8.

My Bag

"His lord said to him, 'Well done, good and faithful servant; you have been faithful over a few things, I will make you ruler over many things. Enter into the joy of your lord.'"
Matthew 25:21 NKJV

Jesus tells a parable of what the kingdom of heaven can be akin to. He describes a master having three servants whom he entrusts bags of silver to, each according to their abilities. One servant is given five bags of silver, another two, and the last servant one. The servants given more than one bag each invested their bags of silver and gained a return, but the servant entrusted with only one bag, driven by fear, buried his bag. When the master returned, he went to each servant to see what they had done with what they were entrusted with. He praised the servants who had a return on their bags of silver but rebuked the servant who had buried his one bag in fear. Notice the focus scripture outlines an outcome based on the action the servants carried out.

- Faithful servants --> The master enlarged their capacity for more --> Servants entered into the joy of the Lord

- Servant driven by fear --> Rebuked by the master --> What was given was taken away

Not only did the faithful servants gain more but also gained access to the joy that was available from the Lord. Joy is available to us when we set out to do what God has called us to do. We enter into the joy of the Lord when we run our own race and steward what has been entrusted to us.

Many times, we get so engulfed in how many bags have been given to others (looking at what everyone else has or what everyone else is doing) that we lose sight of our own bag (our own abilities). We are filled with a fear that we will never measure up to those around us, but the master never meant for the servant with two bags to be able to do what the servant with five bags could do. Nor did he intend for the servant with one bag to accomplish what the servant with two bags did. He gave to each according to their individual abilities.

When we use our gifts and talents, when we steward well the value that is been entrusted to us, not only is our capacity enlarged, but we gain access to the joy of the Lord. There is joy in living out your God-given talents and abilities. There is joy in stewarding what you have been given. There is joy in living out your God-given assignment.

What has kept you from using what you have been entrusted with? Comparison, fear of failure, fear that you cannot do things the way "they" do them? We were not created to be replicas of one another. We have each been entrusted with a value unique to our abilities. Live according to your own gifts and talents and discover the joy the Lord has made available to you.

"Whoever can be trusted with very little can also be trusted with much, and whoever is dishonest with very little will also be dishonest with much." (Luke 16:10)

Recommended Reading: Matthew 25:14-30

Prayer: Dear heavenly Father, thank you for giving me talent and abilities uniquely tailored to me. I pray that you would continue to direct my path that I may not only enter into the joy found in you, but also receive the promotions that can only come through you. Enlarge my tents Father. Increase my joy. In Jesus's name I pray. Amen!

Day 21 Activation

In this parable, we see two faithful servants and one who allowed his fears to keep him from being fruitful with what he had been given. Has anything kept you from stewarding the gifts, talents and abilities God has given you? Fear, comparison, anxiety?

What does *enter into the joy of the Lord* look like for you? Describe.

What are some practical steps you could take to begin moving toward the mark you have been called to attain? List three steps you can take today or throughout the week that would help you journey toward enlarging your capacity for more of what God has already given you.

Eternal Rewards

"The apostles left the high council rejoicing that God had counted them worthy to suffer disgrace for the name of Jesus." Acts 5:41 NLT

The apostles have been arrested by the high council (the Sanhedrin). They are discussing whether they should release the apostles or have them killed for teaching the message of Jesus. A respected pharisee gives several examples of previous movements with followers that eventually died off. He encourages the high council to let the apostles go because if they are acting on their own accord, their movements will soon die off too. However, he warns, if they are acting on behalf of God, the Sanhedrin will find itself fighting against God himself. Collectively, the high council agrees to release the apostles, but not before having them flogged and ordered to never speak in the name of Jesus again.

In our focus scripture, the apostles were arrested and flogged, yet they left rejoicing. Does the word 'joy' come to mind when you think of suffering and disgrace? Not likely. Joy is not typically used to define suffering, pain, rejection, and humiliation. Yet, the apostles rejoiced in their suffering and disgrace. Why is that? What did they know that others did not?

"God blesses those who are persecuted for doing right, for the Kingdom of Heaven is theirs." (Matt. 5:10). The apostles knew that their reward for their present percussion was far greater than any temporal discomfort they would endure. Their reward was kingdom based and, unlike anything on the earth, it was eternal. They could not help but rejoice that the Lord would deem them worthy to receive the

rewards gained through persecution because they were preaching the gospel.

Have you ever been persecuted for your faith? This may not look like a flogging or an imprisonment, but maybe you are left out of a group at work because of your faith. Maybe you have lost relationships in your life because of your decision to follow Christ. Perhaps people talk about you because you seek God in prayer. Rejoice! God blesses those who are persecuted for his sake.

Recommended Reading: Acts 5:26-42

Prayer: Dear heavenly Father, thank you for showing me an example of courage as displayed by the apostles. Thank you, Lord, for reminding me that the world may not always agree with my beliefs, but I have already been approved by you and my rewards are not earthly, but eternal. In your precious name I pray. Amen!

Day 22 Activation

Persecution is a form or rejection. It is centered around hostility toward you, in this case, because of your beliefs. It is safe to say no one likes the feeling of rejection, but realizing the truth outlined in this scripture really sheds a new light on this form of rejection. What has persecution/rejection looked like in your life because of your decision to follow Christ?

How have you experienced this type of persecution in your life? How have you handled it?

Did you know that, in this very moment, you can look back at each and every instance of persecution and rejoice knowing the eternal rewards you have gained? How does that make you feel? Joyous? Redeemed? Describe.

Alignment Births Desire

"Delight yourself in the Lord, and he will give you the desires of your heart." Psalm 37:4 ESV

When we define delight, it is typically associated with a state of being joyful; however, in the context of this scripture, it is referring to alignment. Being aligned simply means being positioned according to the set configuration of something [5]. For instance, every member of a marching band has to be aligned with one another in order to have optimal performance. This is also true for our lives. When we are aligned and positioned in accordance to the will of God for our lives, we too can have optimal performance.

When something is functioning at its optimal level it is moving at its best capacity. When we are aligned with the will of God for our lives, we are living our life at its ultimate ability. We are now partnered with the Creator of the universe. The one who made us in his own image. The one who has fashioned all our days before even one of them came to pass. God knows how we can function at our best, even before we do.

When we delight, when we align, when we partner with the Lord – he begins to birth forth new passions, new ideas, and new desires in our heart. He does not give us the desires of our heart, in the sense of a wish list coming true, but he begins to instill in us, to birth in our hearts new desires that are now aligned with his desires for our lives. When we align ourselves with the Lord, we are not just more efficient because we are now covered by the grace of God, but we are more effective because we are now moving in the gifts the Lord has placed within us.

Notice the focus scripture says to, delight *yourself* in the Lord. Your spouse cannot do it for you, your parents or grandparents cannot do it for you, your neighbors or your co-workers cannot do it for you. You must *choose* to delight *yourself*, align yourself with the Lord. This is the pre-requisite for the promise that follows: *"he will give you the desires of your heart."*

Have you aligned yourself with the Lord? Do you delight in all that he is and all that he wills for your life? Enter into the joy of the Lord! Delight yourself in the Lord! Watch as he plants new desires in your heart that will lead you to places you have never dreamed of.

Prayer: Dear heavenly Father, I delight myself in you. I rejoice in your will for my life. I choose to align my life with the life you have outlined for me. As I position myself before you, I know you will birth desires in my heart that are downloads from your heart for me. In Jesus's name I pray that I receive each and every one of them. Amen!

Day 23 Activation

You may be thinking, "Ok, how do I align myself with the will of God?" I am glad you asked. You simply pray, read the scriptures, and discover what he says about you. As you begin to build your relationship with the Father, you will begin to incline yourself to certain things that perhaps you would have never been drawn to before.

As you seek out his heart in prayer for your life, what is he revealing to you? Write it here so you do not forget.

Are you surprised at what he has shown you? Why or why not?

How can this alignment with the will of the Father birth something in you that has not been birth before? Explain.

God of Hope

"May the God of hope fill you with all joy and peace in believing, so that by the power of the Holy Spirit you may abound in hope." Romans 15:13 NLT

Who do you know God to be? Is he a kind Father? Is he a steadfast figure? Is he the definition of love to you? If you cannot answer *yes* to all of these questions, let me encourage you that he is all of these things and more. In this scripture, Paul gives us insight into the Father as the source of hope. He is addressed as the *'God of hope'*. We know that the scriptures are filled with hope but notice in this scripture, apostle Paul makes the correlation between hope, joy, peace, and belief.

To be *the God of hope* means he is the source of hope. In this hope, there is a transfer that takes place when we find ourselves surrendered to our beliefs in who the scriptures teach us that he is. The God we place our hope in, our Abba Father, has the ability to fill us with all joy and peace because of our faith in his promises. Through this exchange of faith in who our God is, the Holy Spirit is then able to empower us to abound in hope that translates into a joy and peace-filled life.

If you are walking with the Lord, you are filled with the unending hope found in scripture. This hope manifest in our lives as a joy and peace that surpasses all understanding, but why is that? Because we know the secret treasures found in scripture that show us when we are walking with the Lord, when we delight in our Father, he works all things out for our good. That means when the enemy comes against us, when life happens, when the unexpected medical report arrives at our doorstep, our hope is anchored in our God. This is the same *God of hope* that fills us with joy and peace.

If you are not abounding in joy inexplicable, or peace so vast it cannot be understood, you are lacking in your hope in the Lord. When our hope is in the God of hope, the source of hope, no life circumstance should be able to steal your joy. Your joy should be anchored through your hope. If you have no peace, you need to go back to the source of peace. Go back to *the God of hope* who abounds in peace, because your peace is anchored through the hope found in him. Do you see the correlation? When you are anchored to the *God of hope* – joy and peace must follow!

"You will live in joy and peace. The mountains and hills will burst into song, and the trees of the field will clap their hands." (Isaiah 55:12)

Recommended Reading: Romans 8:28, Proverbs 3:5

Prayer: Dear heavenly Father, thank you for being my anchor of hope. Through this hope I find the source of my joy and the source of my peace. King Jesus, thank you for your sacrifice at Calvary that made a way for the Holy Spirit to live in me and empower me to tap into the source of hope that you have left for me to live in. I praise your holy name! Amen!

Day 24 Activation

If you could single out one thing in your life that you constantly run to for hope and comfort, what is it? Search your heart here and be honest with yourself, God already knows anyway. Is it a relationship, friends, family, food, shopping, etc.?

I want to encourage you, if your answer in the previous question was not undoubtably God, that is alright. You can shift your focus from those things that are not God, right back to him. How can you intentionally shift your focus back to the Father?

List the varying ways you see the Father in your life? (Ex.: friend, confidant, comforter, etc.)

Does your list bring you joy? If not, what shift in perspective do you need to make in order to realize that he is a good Father who longs to be in relationship with you every single day? Not just on the mountain tops, but in the valleys too.

Heaven's Party

"In the same way, there is more joy in heaven over one lost sinner who repents and returns to God than over ninety-nine others who are righteous and haven't strayed away!"
Luke 15:7 NLT

Jesus was frequently associated with those who were considered notorious sinners. He was judged and criticized by the pharisees over his involvement with such people. So, Jesus told a parable that gave insight into his purpose for drawing near to those who walked in sin. The parable of the lost sheep is a story of a shepherd who leaves his herd of ninety-nine sheep to go after the sheep that has wandered away from the herd. He tells of how the shepherd rejoices with his friends when he finds his lost sheep and brings it back to the rest of the herd. *"In the same way, there is more joy in heaven over one lost sinner who repents and returns to God than over ninety-nine others who are righteous and haven't strayed away!"*

This parable shows the intricate value Jesus sees in each and every one of us. Regardless of the times we might have wandered away from the light of Christ, or where our current choices place us, Jesus, our shepherd, is drawn to us; seeking to bring us back into the fold. When a sheep wanders away from the herd, it does not stop being a sheep. It is simply a lost sheep. The same is true with us. If we are lost and have wondered away from the Father, it does not make us any less children of God. It just makes us lost children needing to be found.

Think back to a time when you lost something and searched and searched, thinking you would never find it, and then suddenly, there it was. The very thing you had been looking for was now seen and found. How excited where you to find this missing 'thing'? Didn't you rejoice over your found treasure? This is what heaven looks like when a lost child is found by the Shepherd. All of heaven rejoices knowing how much that lost soul needed to be pulled out of the darkness and into the light. There is a celebration over those who were lost and are now found.

Do you have a lost child, a lost friend, spouse, co-worker, or family member? Take heart, the only way to find something is by it being lost. Those ones who are lost will be found and great joy will ripple through the heavens. Do not seize in prayer. Do not relent in your belief for salvation of those who are yet to be found.

"So I say to you, ask, and it will be given to you; seek, and you will find; knock, and it will be opened to you." (Luke 11:9)

Recommended Reading: Luke 15:1-7

Prayer: Dear heavenly Father, the very thought of heaven rejoicing over me is humbling. I can only imagine the joy that swept through the heavens as I found my way into the arms of my Shepherd. Thank you for pursuing me Lord. Thank you for associating yourself with a sinner like me, who once was lost, but now is found. I praise your holy name Jesus! Amen!

Day 25 Activation

As we meditate on this scripture, we can clearly see that the heart of the Father is to bring all souls out of darkness and into the light of Jesus.

Write down the names of those who you are believing God for salvation.

Ask the Father for a scripture (promise) to pray over each individual name. Write the name(s) and their promise(s) here.

You are preparing to throw a party for those who were lost that have been found. What does the party look like? Is there worship, cake, testimonies, etc.? Get creative. Have fun with this. Plan it here.

Did you experience a level of joy by simply planning the celebration? It is a fun reminder of how much our Father rejoices when we finally receive our crown.

Freedom Brings Joy

"And there was great joy throughout the church that day as they read this encouraging message." Acts 15:31 NLT

Some believers who belonged to the sect of the Pharisees began to teach new believers that unless they were circumcised under the Law of Moses, they could not be saved. However, Paul and Barnabas strongly opposed these teachings, reminding believers that salvation was found through the finished work of the cross of Christ Jesus, by faith. Since the dispute was not quickly resolved, the church decided to send both Paul and Barnabas to Jerusalem to bring the matter before the apostles and elders. As they met to discuss the matter, Peter reminded them that the Gentiles received the Holy Spirit just as they (the Jews) had. The Lord made no distinction between the two, so why were they trying to burden the Gentiles with a yoke the Lord had not given.

The apostles and elders concluded that they should not make it more difficult for the Gentiles who were turning to God, thus only imposed certain other restrictions, such as: not eating food offered to idols and abstaining from sexual immorality. As the letter with this message was delivered to the new believers who awaited the response *great joy swept through the church.*

When religious mindsets (as seen here – circumcision under the law) seem to be the underlying agenda, it can leave people feeling oppressed. When people feel burdened and oppressed under a yoke, there is little room for joy to reside. In our focus scripture, we see there was *great joy throughout the church as they read the encouraging message* delivered by the apostles and elders. The message freed the people from a yoke that Jesus had rendered unnecessary. We see clearly, freedom makes room for joy!

Jesus said *"Come to me all you who are weary and heavy burdened, and I will give you rest… For my yoke is easy and my burden is light."* (Matt. 11:28;30). Jesus wants to free us from the oppressive ways of the world. He promises to lift our heavy burdens and bring joy that is found in his love. *"For when we place our faith in Christ Jesus, there is no benefit in being circumcised or being uncircumcised. What is important is faith expressing itself in love."* (Gal. 5:6).

Are you heavy laden today? Are you weary from the oppressive rule of the world? You need more likes on your social media page. You need to make more money. You need a newer car or a bigger house. Jesus wants to take the heavy burdens from you. As you surrender to the law of love found in Christ, you will find joy and freedom from the yoke the world has tried to place over you. Be free from "works" and receive the joy found in his easy yoke.

"We know that a person is made right with God by faith in Jesus Christ, not by obeying the law…For no one will ever be made right with God by obeying the law…For if keeping the law could make us right with God, then there was no need for Christ to die." (Gal. 2:16;21).

Recommended Reading: Acts 15:1-31, Galatians 2:11-21

Prayer: Dear heavenly Father, thank you for the sacrifice of Christ Jesus. Thank you Jesus that you made a way for me to remove the heavy yoke placed upon me by the world and religious mindsets. You have given me a burden that is light and laced with love and joy. I receive it today. In Jesus's name. Amen!

Day 26 Activation

The yoke the world places upon us can look different for all of us. Many times, it can be described as "keeping up with the Jones", while other times it can look like religious practice instead of relationship.

What yoke does Jesus want to set you free from today? Ask him, then write about it here.

For each item on your list, search for scriptures that reveal the truth that sets you free from these "earthly yokes". (Hint: Internet searches are a great place to start. Example: "What does the bible say about [fill in the blank]".)

Describe how being set free from the yokes you have listed above makes room for joy.

Do Not Miss It

"Your love has given me great joy and encouragement because you, brother, have refreshed the hearts of the Lord's people." Philemon 1:7 NIV

In the focus scripture, we see Paul is expressing his gratitude toward Philemon for pouring out his love on God's people. Philemon's willingness to love those around him had a domino effect that generated joy, encouragement, and a refreshing of the heart. In the context of this scripture, the Greek word for refreshing is *anapauo*, which means "to give rest"[2]. As Philemon gave rest to the people of God, joy and encouragement followed. When we are able to minister to those around us, we have made a way for joy and encouragement to enter.

In this scripture we see joy, encouragement, and rest are interconnected and they all stem from love. However, it is not just any love, it is y*our love*, and the unique way you express that love to others. Jesus never spoke a word without an intended purpose. When asked what the greatest commandment was, he said love. *"You must love the Lord your God with all your heart, all your soul, and all your mind. This is the first and greatest commandment. A second is equally important: 'Love your neighbor as yourself.' The entire law and all the demands of the prophets are based on these two commandments."* (Matt.22:37-39). Jesus is telling us that everything hangs on love. If we do not have love, we are missing the gospel message.

Many times, we think we need more money to bring us joy, we need a bigger house, a newer car, a promotion at work, a new relationship, our spouse to give us more attention, and on and on. We can get so caught up with all the things this world has to offer in our attempt to find joy, but the void that we so desperately seek to fill is not found in any of these things. The answer is and always will be Jesus. He is the definition of love expressed in the most extravagant way.

If you are waning in your joy today, let me remind you to love those around you. Love inclusively. Do not leave anyone out. When we love others as Jesus commanded, our returns are joy and encouragement. Do not miss it. Do not miss the message of the gospel. It shouts love and renders joy and encouragement.

Recommended Reading: Philemon 1

Prayer: Dear heavenly Father, thank you for directing me to live a life filled with joy and encouragement through love. Love is powerful. I am so grateful that you have given me the liberty to express the love of Christ to all without exclusion. I pray that you would continue to prune the areas in my life that keep me from loving according to your will. I lift your holy name in praise. Amen!

Day 27 Activation

When we lift others up, we are, unknowingly, setting into motion a principle we see over and over throughout the Bible – you reap what you sow.

Whose life can you sow into today through encouragement? Try to list at least three people you can encourage.

In what ways are you encouraging each name listed above today? Bonus points for creativity. Describe here.

You just described the varying ways you can encourage someone you know, now take a moment to assess your current state of being. How has encouraging others made you feel? Describe it below and take special note of this day. When you are feeling discouraged come back to what you wrote about this day and be encouraged in knowing that God is faithful.

Enjoy Each Play

"The hope of the righteous brings joy, but the expectation of the wicked will perish." Proverbs 10:28 ESV

As we have been studying how joy is intricately found within the scriptures, let's take a moment to note the relation between hope and joy. In this scripture, we see that it is hope that leads to joy. To hope is to expect something, but more than that, to believe that which is expected will be obtained or fulfilled. When we hope in the promises of God, we aren't just wishing and crossing our fingers, we are actively believing that every word spoken is true and will surely come to pass.

You heard the news that your team won the last game they played. You have not watched the game yet, but you have recorded the game and when you get home you will watch it. As you are sitting in your living room, playing back the recording, your team is down by 20 points after the first half. That is a lot of points to be behind, but instead of sitting there nervous and anxious wondering what will happen, you simply enjoy each play. Why? Because you already know the outcome. Regardless of how things look in the middle of the game, you already know your team will win. This is exactly how the life of a believer should be lived.

You are righteous, through Christ, and as an heir of this beautiful inheritance, your story ends in victory. It does not matter what the current score of the game is or how you have performed in previous quarters, you have the victory in Christ. Your salvation through Jesus guarantees your victory. This is the hope of the righteous that leads to joy. The confident expectation that you are in a rigged game, born to win. What joy to know that your circumstances do not determine your outcome. You are content knowing that your circumstances do not have the final say. Jesus had the final say on the cross at Calvary. He defeated death and the grave, so we win! Praise the Lord!

Do you feel like you are behind in life? Perhaps the chapters written in your book, thus far, have not been what you would hope they would be. Today is the day to have a revelation of the goodness of God, the promises that bring guaranteed victories. The truth of his promises that remind us *"Is there anything too hard for our God?"* (Jer. 32:27). No, and you can stand on this confident truth, *"that all things work together for good to those who love God, to those who are the called according to His purpose."* (Rom. 8:28). All things – the good, the bad, and the ugly. God will use every bit of it. The hope of the righteous brings joy because we know our story ends in redeemed victory.

Prayer: Dear heavenly Father, thank you that the cross had the final say. It made a way for me to stand in confident hope knowing that I stand in the righteousness of Christ Jesus. I live with this confident hope that brings a joy that no circumstance can change. It is a joy that springs forth from the promises found in your Word. I praise you for the joy you bring into my life. I praise you Jesus. Amen!

Day 28 Activation

We have all faced a hardship in our life at one time or another. Think back to a time when you faced an unfair situation, a hardship that seemed beyond repair, but as you reflect, you can see the hand of God working. Describe that here.

In what situation are you believing for breakthrough? What promise (scripture) are you praying over that situation?

Since we live in a fallen world, you will likely face hardship along the way. What type of comfort do you sense in knowing that God works all things for good to those who love him? How does this encourage you to face each trying season? Does it inspire an inner joy?

Happenings

"You have put more joy in my heart than they have when their grain and wine abound." Psalm 4:7 ESV

Have you ever noticed people will compliment only what can be seen? You lost weight – compliment. Your outfit is pretty – compliment. New shoes, nice purse, cool hat, beautiful necklace – compliment. They tend to compliment what can be seen with the natural eyes, but have you ever heard someone say, *"Wow, your kindness is on point!" "Your peace is trending." "Your joy is goals."* These are not really compliments we hear in society, yet these are the very things the kingdom of heaven deems worthy of praise.

In our focus scripture we see a contrast between a level of joy found in circumstance and a level of joy sourced from our hearts. The problem with joy derived from circumstance is that it's not really joy at all, its happiness. Happiness is circumstantial, based upon *happenings*. When your spouse "changes", when you buy the big house you have always wanted, when you finally own the latest car model, when you make the grades, when you get the promotion, etc. Go ahead and insert here what you think will make you happy. But do not be fooled, happiness is something that comes and goes as the waves in the sea, but joy – joy is constant, joy is steady, and joy abides. As believers, there is only one single source that has the capacity to fill us with joy. That source is God.

God has placed joy within our hearts, but why is it that some people walk around beaming while others walk around dim. The key word here is *heart*. Our heart is the source that houses our joy. If our heart has been tainted by the things of this world, it will not operate in its fullness.

"Keep your heart with all diligence, for out of it spring the issues of life." (Prov. 4:23). We are warned to guard our heart diligently because the heart creates a flow for our life. If we allow things that do not belong to the kingdom of heaven to take residence within our heart, those things that spring forth from our heart will not line up with the provision God has made for us; a provision to walk in joy.

So, what are things that do not belong that can steal our joy? Comparison, rejection, and fear come to mind. These are just a few, but they are very impactful if we allow them to reside within our heart. We compare ourselves to our friends, relatives, co-workers, or even those we do not know at all. We carry rejection from people who were only meant to come into our lives for a season, but whom we tried to keep for a lifetime. The enemy thrives in the sphere of lies. He whispers, "You will never measure up, you are not enough, no one cares, you cannot make a difference", and many other such lies. He grips you with fear of failure, fear of falling short, etc. He is a liar (John 8:44).

But the Father says, "I have put joy in your heart that supersedes anything circumstantial. Stand in my truth and know that you are more than enough, you were made with a purpose, there is no fear in my love," and many other confirming words. Guard your heart above all else, discover the joy that has been placed within the depths of it, and be the beaming light he has called you to be.

"You are the light of the world." (Matt. 5:14)

Prayer: Dear heavenly Father, thank you that you have already placed within me everything I will ever need to lead a joy-filled life; the extravagant joy that can only be given by you. The joy that abounds to such a degree no measure of abundant *grain* or *wine* could ever surpass it. Thank you Lord. I praise your holy name. Amen!

Day 29 Activation

At times, we have used happiness and joy interchangeably, but they are two different things. Happiness is a fleeting feeling that is attached to a present moment in time, but joy is a constant, steady state of being sourced from the Father's heart.

Is there a situation where you have allowed your joy to be stolen because you led with your feelings? Describe it here.

How can you surrender this situation to the will of the Father and enter into his constant joy?

If we do not learn from previous circumstances we have faced, we are likely to repeat or make similar mistakes. How can you keep yourself from allowing your feelings to lead when a less than favorable situation comes along? (Hint: anchor yourself to a promise found in scripture.)

Restoration Projects

"Restore to me the joy of your salvation and grant me a willing spirit, to sustain me. Then I will teach transgressors your ways, so that sinners will turn back to you."
Psalm 51:12-13 NIV

Have you ever watched one of those restoration shows on TV? Some of them focus on homes, while others focus on cars and vintage items. Regardless of the project, the goal is the same; to bring the item back to its original state. As we relate this to the spiritual journey, restoration typically consists of a team of experts [Father, Son, Holy Spirit] taking something that seems to be broken beyond repair [humanity], utilizing tools to restore it back to its former glory [salvation]. The transformation that takes place is absolutely astounding [fruit of salvation].

Much like these restoration projects, God is looking to restore those who feel they are lost and broken beyond repair. *"For the Son of Man came to seek and save those who are lost"* (Luke 19:10). When Adam and Eve brought about the fall of mankind through their choice to sin, everything seemed to be broken beyond repair, but God had a plan for restoration. Through salvation, we are restored. God is in the business of healing and restoring people. He longs to be good to you. He longs to make you whole. He longs to restore you to your original design. Once you are restored, a transformation happens within you. You then go from needing restoration to supporting restorations for others.

David is asking for restoration that he may bring others to a place of restoration. He asks to be granted a willing spirit that will bear what he cannot in and of himself. The rest of our focus scripture shows us an *"if, then"* condition. Meaning, *if* restored to fullness of joy and given a spirit that will sustain him, *then* he can help bring back those who are lost. We cannot give out what we ourselves do not possess. David knew that if he was going to be able to reach transgressors, he first had to be filled with a joy that could only be found in Christ and a spirit that would sustain him through his assignment.

If you are feeling weary today, ask the Father to restore you. If you are unwilling, ask him to give you a willing spirit that will sustain you for the high calling he has for you. We have all been chosen for something beyond ourselves, but we cannot do it in our own strength. We have all been chosen to display his glory, but we cannot do it without his joy radiating through us.

"Keep on asking, and you will receive what you ask for. Keep on seeking, and you will find. Keep on knocking, and the door will be opened to you." (Matt. 7:7)

Prayer: Dear heavenly Father, sometimes I grow weary along my journey. Restore me with an everlasting joy that abides forever. Sustain me with a willing spirit when I feel like I cannot bear the journey along this road much longer. I know that you are for me. I know that you love me. I know that you have placed joy within me. Remind me that as I ask and seek, you will make a way. I love you Lord. In your mighty name I pray. Amen!

Day 30 Activation

It is natural for us to grow weary as we navigate through this thing called life. As you are given assignments by your Father that seem too great to carry out, remain grounded and rooted in Him knowing that he is the only one who can sustain you through it all.

In what ways has he encouraged and sustained you through different seasons of your life?

As you reflect on the goodness of your heavenly Father, can you see his faithfulness through it all? Can you count it all joy?

The scripture reminds us that we are restored to fullness of joy so we can go back and minister to others. Who can you minister to in this season of your life that perhaps you could not have in a previous season? Reach out to this person and minister to them. Take notes of this encounter here.

Love Them Anyway

"I have loved you even as the Father has loved me. Remain in my love. When you obey my commandments, you remain in my love, just as I obey my Father's commandments and remain in his love. I have told you these things so that you will be filled with my joy. Yes, your joy will overflow! This is my commandment: Love each other in the same way I have loved you." John 15:9-12 NLT

Jesus loves you! *Remain in [his]love.* To remain is to stay, to abide, to dwell, or to inhabit. How do we remain in his love? The scripture gives us the answer – *when [we] obey [his] commandments.* Jesus is telling the disciples they can dwell in his love as they walk in obedience to his commandments. But what does he command? *"Love each other in the same way I have loved you."* Although this sounds quite easy, to love one another, how challenging does it become when the people you are called to love are not so loveable?

Jesus is so wise, all knowing. He knew all the questions we would ask ourselves before we ever knew we would ask them. In all of his wisdom, he left us the answer to this very question of how to love one another. *"Love your neighbor as you love yourself" (*Mark 12:31). We can clearly see; we cannot love others until we first learn to love ourselves. When we stop comparing ourselves, when we stop competing with others, when we stop wishing we had someone else's gift and talents, we can finally love who God created us to be – uniquely made to run our own race in this life.

You have an individual thumbprint. Out of billions of people on the planet, yours is unique to you. No one else has it. This is not just some cute thing we can say to each other, but if we grasp the complexity of it, the intricate detail of it, the uniqueness that it represents, it would lead us to truly embrace who we are and to also love who others were created to be. There is only one *you* in all of creation. Love who that person is, and who that person was born to become.

When you start seeing yourself through the lens Jesus sees you through, you can radically begin loving who you were created to be. You can see others the way Jesus created them to be. If you allowed the power of God's love to rule, there would be no room for hate. So, what happens when you choose love over hate? You enter into the joy of the Lord.

The joy of the Lord is a state of being, not a feeling. It is a joy that cannot be explained, a joy that does not waver based upon circumstance. It is a joy unlike any other. As I was researching *'joy'*, a few synonyms included: treasure, jewel, and prize. Let that sink in. When we choose love over hate, when we choose love over rejection, when we choose love over criticism, we receive a treasure from heaven. We attain a prize from the kingdom of heaven. It is likened to receiving a jewel. That is what joy in the Lord looks like.

Jesus loves us with a radical reckless love despite our behavior, despite our brokenness, and despite our sin nature. He loves us anyway. Loving others can be tough. There are a lot of wounded people in the world. Keep in mind, hurting people can hurt people, but love them anyway – just as Christ loves you, and find yourself entering into the joy of the Lord.

"But God showed his great love for us by sending Christ to die for us while we were still sinners." (Rom. 5:8)

Prayer: Dear heavenly Father, thank you for loving me even in my most unlovable state. I choose to love who you created me to be. Teach me to love those who seem unlovable that my joy may be full, that my joy may overflow. Grow me in love. In Jesus's mighty name I pray. Amen!

Day 31 Activation

To say, to love others as we love ourselves sounds simple enough, right? But what I have experienced with God is that he tends to grow us through trying seasons. Who comes to mind when you think of someone who is not the most "loveable" person to be around?

As today's devotion outlines, *"love them anyway."* How can you express a sincere loving act toward that person who might be difficult to love?

As you reach out to this individual, in whatever way the Lord leads you, please take note in this section how that act has opened a door for you to enter into the joy of the Lord.

Receive Your Inheritance

"I have inherited Your testimonies forever, for they are the joy of my heart." Psalm 119:111 NASB

We typically think of an inheritance as something with monetary value in the form of property, family possessions, or money itself. However, inheritances can also be generational traits, lessons learned, recipes, traditions, etc. Regardless of the form the inheritance comes in, the fundamental truth of an inheritance is that it is free, but it must be received in order to enjoy the benefit of what's been apportioned. It generally holds a level of value, which is based on individual perspective of the person receiving the gift. It is typically followed by the death of someone who held the gift being passed down. Main points here:

·   An inheritance is free, but it must be received.

·   All inheritances have value, but the value is relative to individual perspective.

·   An inheritance is initiated when someone dies.

The Word of God is our inheritance. Salvation is our inheritance. Jesus died at Calvary in order for us to inherit the promises found in the Bible, but like all inheritances, the promises of God must be *received* in order to attain the value found in them. *"For all who are led by the Spirit of God are children of God. For his Spirit joins with our spirit to affirm that we are God's children. And since we are his children, we are his heirs."* (Rom. 8:14; 16; 17). His promises are the unperishable inheritance that holds immeasurable value, but this value can only be seen by those who choose to freely receive the gift given by Jesus's sacrifice.

"*"Testimonies"*", in the context of the focus scripture, is referring to statements or declarations [8]. The Word of God contains the statements that outline our inheritance. The psalmist is declaring the testimonies (Word of God) are his eternal treasures that bring joy to his heart. We see the promises found in the Word have been received and treasured to such a degree, they are the source of his joy. The value of a thing is always relative to our own perspective. The psalmist held the promises found in the Word of God with such esteem they became the source of his joy.

Jesus said, *"Wherever your treasure is, there the desires of your heart will be also."* (Matt. 6:21). The psalmist treasured the Word of God and from his heart surged joy. If the source of our joy is derived from the promises found in his word, this joy cannot be altered, erased or undone. God's promises are eternal giving us access to everlasting joy.

Prayer: Dear heavenly Father, thank you for leaving me such a beautiful inheritance. I treasure every word spoken and every promise given. Your everlasting gifts surpass anything this world could ever offer. I cling to your word and continuously pray for streams of joy to flow from my heart to the hearts of those around me. In Jesus's mighty name I pray. Amen!

Day 32 Activation

As adopted children of God, we are members of a royal family, Jesus's family. Since we are part of his kingdom, we have access to kingdom treasure. What treasure do you have access to that you have not yet received as a child of God or you do not continuously access? (Ex.: joy, peace, rest, health, etc.)

The kingdom of heaven knows no lack. Jesus never stands around with the Father saying, *"Wow, they have so many needs, what are we going to do? We can only handle one thing at a time."* Take all of your needs to the Father. He wants you to walk in the fullness of his goodness.

Your heavenly Father yearns to enrich you in all areas of your life. What needs have you neglected to go to him about? List them here.

As you give your needs to your heavenly Father, search out the Word of God. List the promise/scripture here that aligns with each current unmet need. Pray and believe regarding each need, as you declare the scripture over each need.

Bountiful

"Our hearts ache, but we always have joy. We are poor, but we give spiritual riches to others. We own nothing, and yet we have everything." 2 Corinthians 6:10 NLT

As I read this scripture, everything seemed like a contradiction. How can one have heart ache, yet have joy? Or live in poverty, yet have riches? Or have nothing and everything at the same time? As I surrendered my heart into the hands of the Father, knowing that his ways are not our ways, he began to unfold underlying truths found in this scripture. As we examine the account Paul is sharing with the people at Corinth, we are reminded that God is not bound by our limitations or our senses.

Paul is writing to the people at Corinth and is pleading with them to not forsake the gift of God's goodness and kindness given to them. As Paul endures countless hardship and troubles, he underlines his unfailing faithfulness to the ministry of the gospel. He outlines numerous instances that would bring great grief to anyone under those circumstances, yet he endures – but how?

"You will receive power when the Holy Spirit comes upon you. And you will be my witnesses" (Acts 1:8). In this scripture, Jesus gave us the answer not only to *how* Paul endured, but *why* he endured with joy. We know joy is a state of being and as we are empowered by the Holy Spirit, we now have the ability to operate out of the fruits of the Spirit (Gal. 5:25). The Spirit produces joy (Gal. 5:22). What would seem impossible, in our own strength, becomes possible through the Holy Spirit within us. Despite the heart ache, our joy remains. Despite the hardship, our joy remains.

"We are poor, but we give spiritual riches to others." We see this scripture demonstrated in Acts 3:6, when Peter and John encounter a crippled beggar asking for money. Peter's response to the beggar was not silver and gold, but the miraculous healing power available through the Holy Spirit. In our focus scripture, Paul was poor (in silver and gold), but rich in the power of Christ that brought spiritual riches to those he came across. As he was empowered by the Spirit, he was enabled to witness to others about Christ Jesus.

Paul outlined, that although he owned nothing, he had everything. In Christ, we hold all of the riches, all of the treasures, all of the eternal gifts given to us at salvation. We do not have to own the biggest house, the newest car, the latest fashion to be rich. We can be rich in love, rich in joy, rich in peace, rich in patience, rich in kindness, rich in goodness, rich in faithfulness, rich in gentleness, and rich in self-control, by the Holy Spirit within us.

If your heart aches, be reminded that joy resides within you. Should you experience a worldly lack know that we have a Kingdom economy that knows no lack. We have been empowered through Christ to bring heavenly riches to our world and to those around us. Be a witness today through the power of the Holy Spirit.

Recommended Reading: 2 Corinthians 6:1-10, Acts 3:1-8, Galatians 5:19-26

Prayer: Dear heavenly Father, thank you for giving me more than I deserve. I can easily lose sight of how much I truly hold. Thank you for the bountiful fruits of the spirit you have filled me with that not only blesses me but also blesses those around me. I praise you! In Jesus's name, Amen!

Day 33 Activation

As you journey through this broken world, you may encounter plenty of circumstances were you might feel depleted of things that seem necessary; however, be encouraged in knowing that you have access to a higher capacity, a higher strength, through the Holy Spirit who empowers you.

What seems like a current contradiction in your life, in light of what the scriptures promise?

How does knowing you have access to Holy Spirit power help you change your perspective on the circumstance(s) listed above?

What are some things you could do to remind yourself of the promises found in the Word of God when you face a "faith contradiction"? (Hint: index cards, phone alerts/reminders, etc.) Get creative! What works best for you? Describe here and purpose to do it!

It's a Strategy

"Do not be dejected and sad, for the joy of the Lord is your strength." Nehemiah 8:10b NLT

Dejected is another word for depressed. Have you ever gone through circumstances in your life that left you feeling dejected and grieved? You felt so saddened by your situation or perhaps the situation a friend or loved one was going through that you could physically feel the pain. Whether it manifested through a headache, a stomachache, a loss of appetite, or even a desire to just sleep; you could physically feel the weighty grief of the situation. In our focus scripture, we are given a reason not to be sad and dejected, *"The joy of the Lord is [our] strength."*

Many times, we feel we are being attacked in our marriages, our friendships, and even in our relationships with our family members and co-workers; believing that the enemy is after those things, but what if he is simply using those things to steal your joy? What if he knows the joy of the Lord is your strength and he wants you weakened in order to strike? What am I saying here? Maybe the thing he seems to be after is not really the thing he is after. What if the thing he is after is your joy? Notice the antidote for sadness and dejection is not simply joy, but the *strength* found in that joy.

"A joyful heart is good medicine, but a broken spirit dries up the bones." (Prov. 17:22). We see in this proverb how a downcast, dejected spirit can create a physical affliction to our bodies *(dries up the bones)*. While a heart filled with the joy found in the Lord produces the antidote *(good medicine)*. Do not let the enemy take your joy. He is after your strength. It is a strategy for him to strike you in a

weakened state. Hold on to the joy of the Lord because it is your strength.

If you are feeling dejected today, rejoice in the Lord! If you feel like you do not have the strength to make it through the challenging circumstance, hold on to the joy found in the Lord – it will strengthen you. Do not allow the enemy to creep in through your circumstances to distort what has already been given to you – the joy found in your faith. He knows your joy is a source of strength rooted in Christ. Do not let the devil win.

"Don't be discouraged, for I am your God. I will strengthen you and help you." (Isa. 41:10b)

Prayer: Dear heavenly Father, I live in awe of your goodness. Not only do you love me and give me all I need, but you have set up ways to strengthen me when I am feeling consumed by the worries of this world. You remind me to rejoice in you knowing this will be refreshing to my soul, a strengthening of my body. I praise you Father. In Jesus's beautiful name I pray. Amen!

Day 34 Activation

Realize the enemy is after your strength and he will use circumstances, people, even your own thoughts to bring destruction.

Can you identify a circumstance, relationship, or any thoughts the enemy has used to rob you of your joy?

When you are faced with these types of situation, immediately identity the strategy being used to rob you of your joy. He is really after your strength. Now that you have identified his ploy, how can you handle these circumstances differently?

Find a promise in scripture that brings you back to a place of joy, victory, and rest. Write it down here and try to memorize it. Remember, the Word of God is a weapon. Use your weapon when you come under attack.

Ah-Ha!

"And these things we write to you that your joy may be full."
1 John 1:4 NKJV

Have you ever had an *ah-ha* moment? When all of a sudden what seemed clouded and muddy became crystal clear. You grasped something at a new level that elevated your understanding of the matter. This newfound knowledge or revelation left you feeling included no longer ousted or excluded. Our focus scripture is attempting to outline this very thing for the believers John is writing to.

John's letter is written in an effort to dispel false teachings that were beginning to spread by heretic rival groups. The letter was intended to foster fellowship amongst the believers he had previously ministered to. As John shares his own personal encounters he experienced with Jesus, he reminds believers of the truth of who Christ is. *"He is the Word of life. This one who is life itself was revealed to us, and we have seen him. And now we testify and proclaim to you that he is the one who is eternal life."* (1 John 1:2-3).

John is saying, "Don't believe the lies these others are trying to convince you of. I've seen him. I've touched him. I've walked with him. He is the one we have been searching for. He has been revealed to us." As he is reaching out to the believers, imploring them to hold on to what is true, John declares, *"these things we write to you that your joy may be full."*

When we are tethered to the truth of who Christ Jesus is – the Word of Life, the one who is life itself, the one who is eternal life – it is there that our joy is made full, made complete, and made whole. We find our joy in Christ Jesus when we come to our *ah-ha* moment of who Christ really is. If your joy is in short supply today, go back to Christ. Go back to the truth of who he is. He is life itself. He is the eternal one. He is your savior. He is your friend. He is your advocate. He is your source of unchanging joy. Search for him and you will always find him.

"Seek, and ye shall find." (Matt. 7:7)

Recommended Reading: 1 John 1:1-3

Prayer: Dear heavenly Father, thank you for being my everything. I am so grateful for the things revealed to me. As I discover these ah-ha moments with you, I know that my joy is that much more complete. I praise you. In Jesus's name. Amen!

Day 35 Activation

As I grew in my relationship with the Lord, I realized I grew up practicing religion my entire childhood. In truth, I had no knowledge of anything found in the scriptures outside of the ritualistic nature of what I was taught as a child. Thank God he comes to set us free with the truth found in the scriptures.

Look back to a time in your life when you encountered an *ah-ha* moment that dispelled a false truth, taught solely by religion and not by the Word of God? Describe it here.

How did this newfound revelation bring you freedom and set you free from a "religious idea"?

Freedom and joy go hand in hand. Describe how the truths found in the Word of God have brought joy into your life.

Role Model

"Looking unto Jesus, the author and finisher of our faith, who for the joy that was set before Him endured the cross, despising the shame, and has sat down at the right hand of the throne of God." Hebrews 12:2 NKJV

Do you remember the person you looked up to when growing up, or the one you considered a good role model for your family? We have all had someone, whether in our childhood or as adults. We admired them for qualities they embodied, or a tremendous impact they had on the world. Regardless of the angle, they displayed something that made us want to be more like of them.

"Looking unto Jesus", is our queue to look at the example displayed by our Lord. Jesus was the ultimate role model to live our lives by. He not only showed mercy, grace, love, kindness, compassion, and infinite wisdom (amongst many other things), but he endured with immeasurable selflessness. How was it possible for Jesus, the Son of God, to hang on a cross, while he could have easily called down angel armies to rescue him? Our focus scripture gives us some insight; *"who for the joy that was set before Him endured the cross."*

Jesus showed us that joy was not a feeling but a state of being. As he hung on the cross, Jesus still ministered. As a criminal hung beside him, Jesus said to him, *"Truly, I say to you, today you will be with me in paradise."* (Luke 23:43). He chose to focus on the joy that would follow his sacrifice. He looked to what would be accessible through the price he paid. Salvation made available to all mankind – the joy set before Jesus. The scripture does not tell us Jesus pretended it was easy. It does not say Jesus pretended not to *"despise the shame*", **but** *"for the joy that was set before him, he endured."*

Is your focus on your hardship or is it on the promise on the other side of it? Do you look to social media, your spouse, family, friends, or perhaps a career to bring you joy? I want to encourage you to look unto Jesus, who is the source of all joy. Keep your heart set on Jesus and allow him to do what only he can do. You do not have to pretend your circumstance is easy. You do not have to embrace the shame – it's ok to despise it. In the midst of your storms, in the midst of your setbacks, and every challenge you may be faced with, if you look unto Jesus – the author and finisher of your faith – you will find joy. *"Seek, and you will find"* (Matt. 7:7).

"For to this you were called, because Christ also suffered for us, leaving us an example, that you should follow His steps" (1 Peter 2:21).

Prayer: Dear heavenly Father, there are no words that could ever express my gratitude for the sacrifice that was made on the cross for me. Jesus you chose to die for me, while I was still a sinner. I praise you Lord. I thank you for the infinite wisdom you left for me, through your Word, and all the examples you left behind for me to study, learn, and follow. I choose to set my eyes on you through every circumstance, good and bad. I know you are in the midst of all of them with me. I praise you Jesus. Amen!

Day 36 Activation

Is there something in your life that seems like a hardship that would benefit from a shift in your perspective? List it here.

You could easily focus on the pain of a hardship, but what if you focused on the "joy set before you." In other words, focus on the benefit of overcoming the hardship. What does that look like for you? Reference your list above and write down the benefit of overcoming each scenario.

Jesus is the ultimate role model for kingdom living. How have you modeled your life after the Lord and how can that be improved or sustained?

All Seasons Change

"Weeping may endure for a night, but joy comes in the morning." Psalm 30:5b NKJV

Our focus scripture reminds us not only that all seasons change, but all seasons come to an end. While we are going through the season in life that we will classify as a winter season – it's dark, cold, nothing seems to grow, and it seems the sun will never shine again, we feel like our weeping is unending but winter eventually gives way to spring. The winter snow begins to melt, signaling to us spring is around the corner. We know that life begins to change and grow in the spring season. The waters that pour in the spring rain are the very waters that fuel growth for new life in the new season.

The water of spring serves to bring the beauty we enjoy in the summer. As much as we enjoy walking under the warmth of the sun and letting the radiant rays of the sunshine hit our skin, inevitably summer eventually gives way to the changing leaves that signal the fall season has arrived. As beautiful as the changing leaves and the cool fall breeze may be, when the leaves begin to disappear, we know winter is approaching again. No one season is better than the other. They are equally valuable, but uniquely purposed. If we learn to discern the changes in our lives as changing seasons, we will learn to embrace the different seasons that we will inevitably find ourselves in.

While weeping may be akin to a winter season – everything seems cold and dark; nothing seems to be growing, rest assured, no season is ever wasted. As we lay down for rest every night, we trust, regardless of life's circumstances, the sun will rise the next day. In this same way, we have the assured confidence that God will not waste your tears. You will not go through a winter season without hope of ever seeing the sunshine again. Weeping may be your companion in the nighttime, but joy will rise with you in the morning. How can you be so sure?

Our focus scripture is the very assurance of this promise. The promises of God are unchanging. They are unmovable and irrevocable. If you find yourself in a winter season, let me encourage you today that spring is around the corner. If you just keep your eyes on Jesus, keep your hope anchored to the one who cannot be moved, your weeping will give way to the joy that resides within your heart. Do not wait for the miracle. Worship the Lord now and allow him to work the miracle in his perfect timing. As you worship him, you will find yourself standing right at the center of the joy that can only be found in him.

Prayer: Dear heavenly Father, thank you for the changing seasons of my life. I know with each season comes growth and blessings. Help me to keep my eyes fixed on you. As I walk through the winter seasons in life, I declare I am firmly anchored to my hope found in you. I praise you Lord. Amen!

Day 37 Activation

Describe a winter season in your life.

How did your winter season change? If you are still in this winter season, how have you seen God work through this current season in your life?

God is faithful! How have you seen the hand of God in your life regarding this scripture, *"weeping may endure for a night, but joy comes in the morning"*? As you see God's faithfulness, let this blessed assurance fill your heart with joy. Capture this moment here.

Flesh or Spirit

"But the Holy Spirit produces this kind of fruit in our lives: love, joy, peace, patience, kindness, goodness, faithfulness, gentleness, and self-control. There is no law against these things!" Galatians 5:22-23 NLT

In nature, a tree is recognized by the fruit it produces. An apple tree labeled as an orange tree will still produce apples and not oranges. Despite what it is labeled, the tree produces what its seed contains. The same is true of Christians. Many can be labeled as Christ followers, but the fruit that is produced defines the validity of that claim.

Fruit, in the Bible, refers to behavioral characteristics. *"You can identify them by their fruit, that is, by the way they act."* (Matt. 7:16a). We may know many who claim to be followers of Christ, but how do they behave under duress. How do they behave when things are not going their way? Do they respond in outbursts of anger and seek to relieve their circumstantial reality through selfish means, or do they hold on to their peace, remain faithful, and continue to display love in the face of unfair circumstances?

Behavioral characteristics reveal what we yield to – the Spirit or the flesh. Our focus scripture reveals the nine fruits produced by the Holy Spirit. Notice the fruit is produced by the Spirit and not by our own effort. If we read a few verses before our focus scripture, we discover how, in contrast to the Spirit, the flesh can produce fruit as well. *"When you follow the desires of your sinful nature, the results are very clear: sexual immorality, impurity, lustful pleasures, idolatry, sorcery, hostility, quarreling, jealousy, outbursts of anger, selfish ambition, dissension, division, envy, drunkenness, wild parties, and other sins like these."* (Gal. 5:19-21).

We see a stark contrast between the fruits of the flesh and the fruits of the Spirit. Our sinful nature brings about destruction, while the Spirit promotes life and unity. Many times, we begin to work out of our own flesh, while striving for the things the Spirit freely produces. We seek love by turning to sexual and lustful desires but as we surrender to the Spirit, the Spirit freely produces love. We seek more joy in our lives and turn to selfish ambition, believing that once we have this thing or that achievement, we'll be happy, but the reality is that if we want joy in our lives all we have to do is surrender our agendas to the Lord and he'll fill us with joy to overflow.

If the things we seek have already been purchased for us, how then does the Spirit overcome our sinful nature? *"Those who belong to Christ Jesus have nailed the passions and desires of their sinful nature to his cross and crucified them there."* (Gal. 5:24). What have you been striving to attain in your own efforts that the Lord has already purchased for you? Are you striving to attain more peace, more love, more joy, or more self-control? The Lord has already purchased these things for you and more.

"Since we are living by the Spirit, let us follow the Spirit's leading in every part of our lives" (Gal. 5:25).

Recommended Reading: Galatians 5:19-26

Prayer: Dear heavenly Father, thank you for purchasing everything I would ever want and need. Thank you that I do not have to strive for love, you freely give it. Thank you that I do not have to strive for joy, you have already given it. I praise your glorious ways. In Jesus's mighty name I pray. Amen!

Day 38 Activation

What an amazing revelation to know that when the battle ensues between the flesh and the Spirit, if we **choose** to surrender to the **Spirit**, we receive life-giving fruit.

In what areas of your life have you allowed the flesh to lead, while looking for fruit produced by the Spirit?

A great way to prepare for a battle is to not only know your strengths, but also know your weaknesses. What are some "triggers" in your life that cause you to give in to the flesh?

Since you have identified some triggers in your life, what is one way you can promote the Spirit's victory over the flesh in the next wrestling match that presents itself in your life? (Hint: worship, scripture, prayer, surrender, etc.)

Mourning into Dancing

"You have turned my mourning into joyful dancing. You have taken away my clothes of mourning and clothed me with joy." Psalm 30:11 NLT

As I read this scripture, the first thing that came to mind was "how"? How does the Lord turn my mourning into dancing? How can he take away my rags and give me glorious joy? In short, how can he bring *deliverance* into my life? Deliverance means to be saved or rescued from something or someone [7]. When the psalmist, David, wrote this portion of scripture, he was reminiscent of the distress he had previously been in. The Lord rescued him from his enemies, he restored him to health, and he saved him from the pit of the grave. David was exclaiming that the Lord turned all of the afflictions he faced into joyful dancing because he delivered him out of them all.

His enemies did not triumph over him. As he cried out to the Lord, the Lord restored his health and kept him from falling into the pit of death. David's response was to make a joyful dance, exalting his holy name. When the Israelites were delivered out of Egypt, *"Miriam the prophetess, Aaron's sister, took a tambourine in her hand, and all the women followed her with tambourines and dancing."* (Exod. 15:20). God turned their mourning into joyful dancing through deliverance.

If you are thinking, "Well he has not delivered me yet. I am still in the midst of my pain. How can my mourning be turned into joyful dancing?" *"For every child of God defeats this evil world, and we achieve this victory through our faith"* (1 John 5:4). That is deliverance. Rejoice! Your circumstances may not always look like what you know to be true. If you are still in the midst of a trial, be encouraged, you are a child of God; therefore, you have defeated the things of this evil world, through Christ. Your deliverance has already been sealed.

Even when we do not see how things are going to work out or cannot make sense of what we are going through, we know that God is faithful to his word. He will turn your mourning into dancing. He will take away your cloak of heaviness and give you joy in exchange. Believe and declare his promises over your life and watch him deliver you through each trying season. As your pain meets his deliverance you will experience the joy that can only be found in his faithfulness. Rejoice!

Recommended Reading: Psalm 30

Prayer: Dear heavenly Father, I rejoice in knowing you have delivered me from the hands of the enemy. As I face trials and hardships in my life that I wish weren't part of my story, I thank you Lord in knowing that you will continue to deliver me through each one. I rejoice in the truth – you are who you say you are. You are my Lord, my Savior, my Friend, my Counselor, and my all and all. True joy is found in knowing who you are. I praise your holy name. Amen!

Day 39 Activation

Through the many years I have walked with the Lord, I have learned that he is, indeed, oh so faithful! I can look back over my life and see all of the places where he guided and held me through tough seasons. Our focus scripture is such a beautiful reminder of his nature – faithful and true.

Recall a time in your life where the Lord showed himself faithful and true. Describe below.

How does the memory described above cause you to rejoice?

When life brings tribulation, remember his Word, reflect upon his faithful nature – he will surely turn your mourning into dancing, again and again. Write something here, based upon scripture, that you can look back on during difficulties, for needed encouragement.

What Are You Ingesting?

"Your words were found, and I ate them, And Your word was to me the joy and rejoicing of my heart; For I am called by Your name, O LORD God of hosts." Jeremiah 15:16 NKJV

When we eat something, the intended purpose is to nourish our bodies. The prophet Jeremiah is making a parallel to food and the Word of God. As we see the parallel between food and the Word, we know the Bible is not something we can physically consume. However, if we intake its written word, it can provide nourishment to our souls. As Jeremiah ingested the Word, it became joy to him. Furthermore, he received a revelation of the Lord and his own identity. How?

In the natural, there are varying foods and flavors. Even amongst the varying foods and flavors are the varying taste palates we each have. An orange might not taste exactly the same to you as it does to me. The same is true with the Word of God. The same scripture can be read by all of us, but the Holy Spirit will cause it to reach each of us in a unique way – the way our souls need it. In parallel to food, each food group is intended to satisfy a particular nutrient our bodies need, much like the Word of God, it ministers to the places in our souls that need to be reached.

As the Word of God goes forth, and we choose to intake it, it does more than just check off our box for the "Word of the day." As the Lord continues to reveal the places within us that need to be surrendered to him, in order to be touched by him, the Word is strategically performing surgery. When we allow ourselves to be enveloped by God's goodness, we begin to experience a joy that can only be found in his arms. As Jeremiah ate the Word, it became to him a joy and a delight. When something *"becomes"*, it does not start off as what it turns into. It is a transformation process. When we find the Word and eat it, it begins a transformation process within us that can only be accomplished through ingesting the Word of God.

When we allow this transformation process to take place, we not only receive the joy found in Christ, but we begin to discover who we are in Christ. The prophet received joy and a delight in his heart because he realized, *"For I am called by Your name, O Lord God of hosts."* When we realize we are called by name by the Creator of the universe, the God of heaven's armies (God of hosts), we simply cannot remain the same.

What have you allowed your soul to ingest? Are you feeding it with the Word of God or are you feeding it with the things of this world? Are you allowing the Word of God to reveal that you are called by His name, or are you allowing social media and others to call you by the names they see fit? Let's purpose to take inventory today and embrace the truths found in his word that will lead our hearts to rejoice.

Prayer: Dear heavenly Father, thank you for choosing to call me by your name. I surrender knowing that true joy can only be found in knowing your truth, in ingesting your Word. I know you have called me, O God of heaven's armies. Strengthen my resolve to remain in your word, to eat your Word, that it may become the joy of my life. In Jesus's mighty name I pray. Amen!

Day 40 Activation

Consumption is not solely related to food. Yes, we consume food, but we also consume the news, social media feeds, movies, music, etc.

If you took an inventory of your daily consumption, would you be full of the Word of God, or full of social media, culture, and the things of this world? No condemnation here. Be honest. We cannot be healed or redirected from the things we do not identify.

Make a list of all the labels the world has placed on you. (Ex.: not enough, need more followers, too old, too young, overweight, etc.)

When the world labels you something other than what your heavenly Father has called you, rejoice in knowing the truth found in his Word. Reject those things that are not of him. Make a list of the labels God has placed on you that are contrary to the list you have written above. (Ex.: redeemed, chosen, loved, etc.). Rejoice!

Notes

1. "25 Amazing Facts About the Human Brain You Should Probably Memorize," Inc., June 14, 2017, https://www.inc.com/john-brandon/25-amazing-facts-about-the-human-brain-you-should-probably-memorize.html (accessed July 10, 2020)

2. Bible Study Tools, s.v, "Refresh", https://www.biblestudytools.com/dictionary/refresh-refreshing/ (accessed July 7, 2020)

3. "Calm your Anxious Heart," Harvard Health Publishing Harvard Medical School, October 1, 2019, https://www.health.harvard.edu/heart-health/calm-your-anxious-heart (accessed June 30, 2020)

4. "This is How Joy Affects Your Body," Healthline, June 27, 2018 https://www.healthline.com/health/affects-of-joy#2 (accessed June 15, 2020)

5. Webster's Dictionary, s.v. "Align", https://www.merriam-webster.com/dictionary/align (accessed July 10, 2020)

6. Webster's Dictionary, s.v. "Anxiety", https://www.merriam-webster.com/dictionary/anxiety (accessed June 30, 2020)

7. Webster's Dictionary, s.v. "Deliverance", https://www.merriam-webster.com/dictionary/deliverance (accessed July 22, 2020)

8. Webster's Dictionary, s.v. "Testimony", https://www.merriam-webster.com/dictionary/testimony (accessed June 27, 2020)

9. "What does anxiety feel like and how does it affect the body?" Medical News Today, July 18, 2018, https://www.medicalnewstoday.com/articles/322510 (accessed June 10, 2020)

10. "What to Know About Anxiety," Medical News Today, January 11, 2020 https://www.medicalnewstoday.com/articles/323454#what-is-anxiety (accessed June 16, 2020)

About the Author

Moved with a heart to fulfill the great commission and bring the Word of God to all yearning hearts, Jessica writes from a place of simplicity. Her heart is to introduce scripture with everyday living in mind. To bring simplicity that allows all hearts to receive while keeping the weighty value the Word of God brings.

A former Interrogator, with a very colorful career, Jessica gained an invaluable analytical background, that is now Holy Spirit inspired as she combs through the Word of God for insight – hidden treasure in plain sight. As a military wife of 15 years, Jessica has had the privilege of living across many states and meeting amazing people all along the way who have enriched her journey. Born and raised in Southern California and a mom of three amazing children, Josue, Jessebella, and Max – they keep her inspired, as she continuously searches out the Father's heart.

When she's not writing, she's taking in God's natural beauty enjoying beautiful hikes or is curled up with a good book on a cozy couch.

For weekly inspiration visit www.reflectingontheword.com

Made in the USA
Monee, IL
10 July 2023